Children's
AMAZING PLACES
Encyclopedia

Author: Robert Hamilton

Consultant: Fiona Waters

© 2009 by Parragon Books Ltd

This 2010 edition published by Sandy Creek, by arrangement with Parragon.

Sandy Creek
122 Fifth Avenue
New York, NY 10011

ISBN-13: 978-1-4351-1912-3

Printed in Indonesia

10 9 8 7 6 5 4 3 2 Lot

Children's
Amazing Places
Encyclopedia

Discover famous wonders of the world

Robert Hamilton

Sandy Creek

Festival Pier

CONTENTS

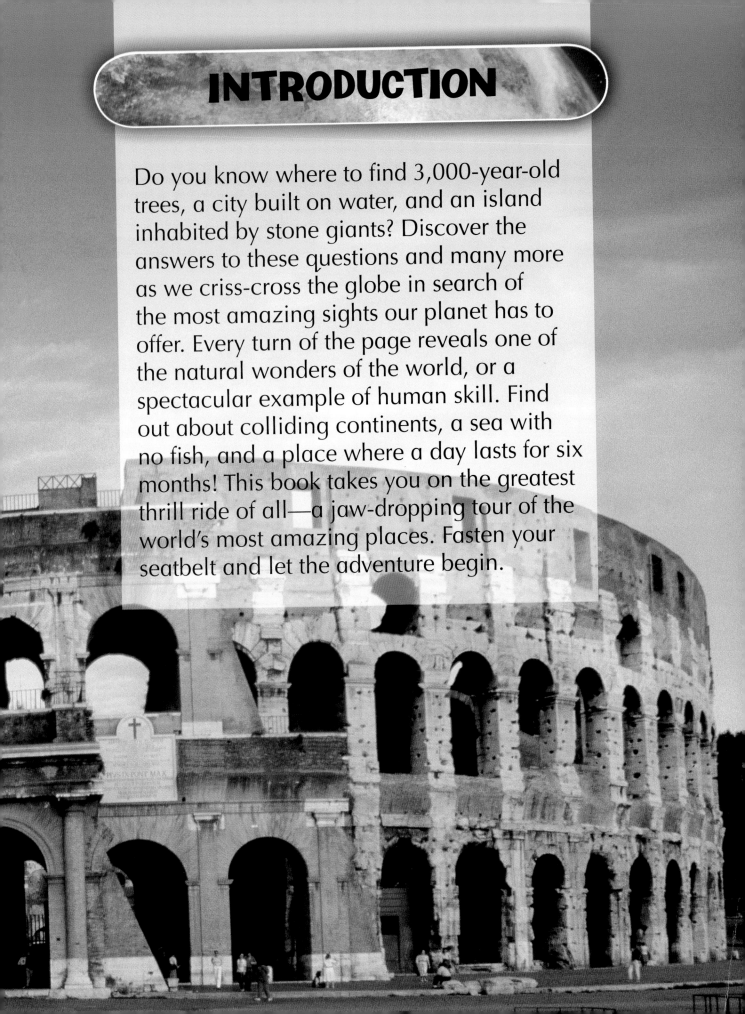

INTRODUCTION

Do you know where to find 3,000-year-old trees, a city built on water, and an island inhabited by stone giants? Discover the answers to these questions and many more as we criss-cross the globe in search of the most amazing sights our planet has to offer. Every turn of the page reveals one of the natural wonders of the world, or a spectacular example of human skill. Find out about colliding continents, a sea with no fish, and a place where a day lasts for six months! This book takes you on the greatest thrill ride of all—a jaw-dropping tour of the world's most amazing places. Fasten your seatbelt and let the adventure begin.

FANTASTIC FEATURES

The forces of nature have created some of the most spectacular sights on Earth. In this chapter, you will find out about mighty waterfalls, rocks that are two billion years old, and mountains carved by rivers of ice. You will learn about a sea with no fish, and a continent that is slowly being torn apart. Find out about the coldest place on the planet, where a cup of coffee would freeze immediately, and about how a volcano formed a staircase fit for a giant!

Antarctica

Antarctica is an ice desert, often called the "last great wilderness." No ship reached Antarctica until 1820, making it the last continent to be discovered. This is because the Southern Ocean surrounding Antarctica is so big and its stormy seas make it difficult to cross.

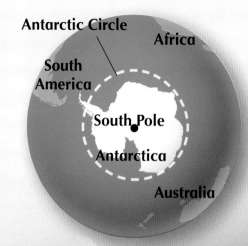

Naming Antarctica

People knew about the Arctic, the area around the North Pole, and guessed there must be land at the southern tip of the Earth too. They called it the Antarctic—"the opposite of the Arctic." Unlike the Arctic, which is a frozen ocean, Antarctica is a continent—a vast area of land covered in ice.

Icebergs

The ice in Antarctica is over 2$\frac{1}{2}$ miles thick in places and it is always moving. Rivers of ice, called glaciers, flow toward the coast, traveling at a speed of 32 feet per year. When the ice reaches the ocean, huge blocks sometimes break off. These floating islands of ice are called icebergs.

Scientific research

Scientists from all over the world come to Antarctica to study changes in sea levels, weather, and climate. Although it is cold, visitors have to take care not to get sunburned because the snow and ice reflect most of the Sun's rays.

Antarctic animals

Around 98 percent of Antarctica is covered in ice. In summer penguins and other birds gather on the small amount of bare rock to feed and to have their young. The area is safe from predators and there is plenty of food in the ocean.

Crabeater seal

Did You Know?
Antarctica has the lowest temperature ever recorded, -128°F. A cup of coffee made with freshly boiled water would freeze immediately in that temperature.

Giant's Causeway

The extraordinary shape of these rocks in Northern Ireland amazed everyone when they were discovered 300 years ago. At first no one was sure if they were natural or artificial. The blocks of stone looked like a huge staircase or causeway, and people made up stories about a giant who built it to settle an argument with a rival across the sea.

Top Facts

- There are around 40,000 columns in the Causeway. Some of them are 39 feet high.

- There are similar rock formations on the Scottish island of Staffa. These supported the myth of the giant building a causeway across the sea.

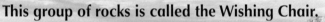
This group of rocks is called the Wishing Chair.

Volcanic rocks

By 1800 scientists had proved that the columns in the Giant's Causeway were formed after a volcano erupted around 60 million years ago. When the lava cooled it cracked and broke up, forming a type of rock called basalt.

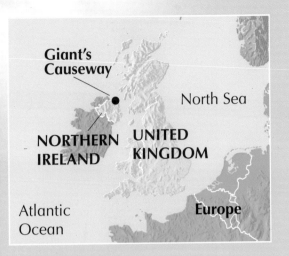

Giant's Causeway

North Sea

NORTHERN
IRELAND

UNITED
KINGDOM

Atlantic
Ocean

Europe

The legend of Finn MacCool

Legend says that the giant Finn MacCool's rival, an even bigger giant called Benandonner, came across the sea on the causeway to fight him. Finn's wife wrapped Finn in a blanket and put him in a cradle. When Benandonner saw the "baby" and imagined how big its father must be, he turned and ran, ripping up the causeway as he went.

Did You Know?

Many visitors sit in the Wishing Chair, a stone seat that is said to have been made for the giant Finn MacCool when he was a boy.

Crossing the sea

The Carrick-a-Rede Bridge is only a few minutes away from the Giant's Causeway. It links mainland Ireland to the tiny island of Carrick. The narrow rope bridge spans 65 feet and there is a 98-foot drop onto the rocks below.

The Matterhorn

The Matterhorn's pyramid shape has made it famous all over the world. It is in the Swiss Alps, near the border with Italy. The Matterhorn is 14,692 feet high —less than half the height of Mount Everest, the world's highest mountain. It isn't even the highest peak in the Alps, but its pyramid shape has drawn climbers to it for over 150 years.

North Sea

Europe

SWITZERLAND

●Matterhorn

Did You Know?

The four sides of the Matterhorn face the four compass points—north, south, east, and west.

Top Facts

- A Matterhorn ride was one of the first attractions built when Disneyland opened in California in 1955. This rollercoaster ride is exactly 100 times smaller than the real mountain.

- The name "Matterhorn" comes from two German words, meaning "meadow peak."

Early mountaineers

In the 1800s the Matterhorn inspired fear in climbers, and there were many failed attempts before the summit was reached. Many tried to go up the southern face, which looks easy from below but is really very difficult. A British climber called Edward Whymper thought that the northern face might be an easier route. He led a party of seven people to the top in 1865. Unfortunately, on the way down four of the climbers fell to their deaths.

The mountain today

Reaching the top of the Matterhorn is a lot easier today. A cable car takes climbers to the foot of the mountain, and there are ropes and ladders along the way to the peak. Climbers usually spend the night at a hut situated at 10,500 feet, then set out for the summit early the next morning. This allows them time to reach the summit and return to safety before the afternoon cloud or stormy weather arrives. Thousands climb the Matterhorn every summer, but there are many dangers. Rockfalls and avalanches kill several people every year.

The Dead Sea

The Dead Sea, which is surrounded by land, has the saltiest water in the world. In some places it is 10 times saltier than normal seawater. No animals or plants can live there, which is why it got its name.

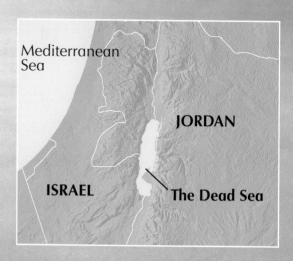

Mediterranean Sea

JORDAN

ISRAEL

The Dead Sea

Did You Know?

The Egyptian queen Cleopatra visited the Dead Sea in the first century B.C. to try its healing waters.

The salt makes the water very dense. You float on the surface of the Dead Sea as if you were on an airbed.

A healthy place

The Dead Sea is a popular health resort. The mud on the shore is rich in minerals and is said to be good for the skin, so many visitors smear mud over their skin. The air around the sea is clean and can help people with breathing problems such as asthma.

Salt crystals

Water from surrounding rivers flows into the Dead Sea. A lot of the water evaporates under the hot Middle Eastern sun, leaving white salt crystals on the shore.

Top Facts

- The Dead Sea is the lowest place on Earth. It is over 1,300 feet below sea level.

- The Dead Sea is sinking by around 12 inches every year because it lies on a thin part of the Earth's crust.

- Scientists think the Dead Sea could dry up in the next 50 years because the river water that flows into it is being taken and used for drinking water and for industry.

The Dead Sea Scrolls

In 1947 a shepherd looking for his animals discovered some jars in an isolated cave near the Dead Sea. These jars contained ancient scrolls. The scrolls (shown above) were mainly made from animal skins and on them were written religious texts. Over the next few years more than 800 scrolls of different sizes were found, the largest being an amazing 26 feet long.

The Great Rift Valley

The Great Rift Valley in East Africa is a giant crack in the Earth's crust. The crust is made up of about 20 huge plates that fit together like a giant jigsaw, and the continents and oceans sit on top of them. These plates move around, and the places where they meet are called fault lines. Mountain ranges and deep valleys form along these lines, and earthquakes and volcanoes are common. The Great Rift Valley lies on one of these fault lines.

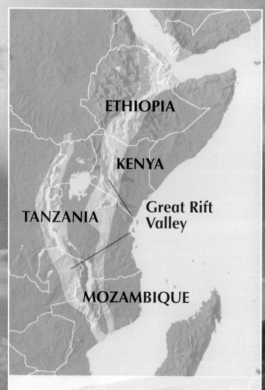

ETHIOPIA

KENYA

Great Rift Valley

TANZANIA

MOZAMBIQUE

Did You Know?
Scientists think that humankind first appeared in the Great Rift Valley. The oldest human bones have been found there.

Ol Doinyo Lengai Volcano in Tanzania

Most fault lines are at the bottom of the oceans. The Great Rift Valley is one of the few that appear on land. It is nearly 3,100 miles long, stretching from southwestern Asia to Mozambique in East Africa.

The valley

The flat plains that make up the floor of the valley are between 30 miles and 60 miles wide. These vast plains are full of wildlife, especially in the national parks of Tanzania and Kenya. Some of the world's largest lakes are found in the valley, including Lake Victoria. At the edges of the valley steep cliffs often rise hundreds of yards into the air.

A herd of elephants makes its way across the plains below Mount Kilimanjaro.

Top Facts

- Africa's highest mountain, Kilimanjaro, is in the Great Rift Valley. Its 19,000-foot-high peak is covered in snow all year round, even though it is near the Equator.

- Africa will eventually split in two along the line of the Great Rift Valley, though it may not happen for thousands of years.

Volcanoes

There are around 30 volcanoes along the Great Rift Valley, and also many boiling hot springs. Volcanoes are found at weak spots in the Earth's crust. As the crust is pulled apart, hot, melted rock from deep underground rises to the surface.

The River Nile

The Nile is the world's longest river. It stretches around 4,000 miles from its source in central Africa to the north coast of Egypt, where it flows into the Mediterranean Sea. Before it reaches the sea, the Nile splits into several channels. This part of the river is called the Nile Delta.

Mediterranean Sea

Nile Delta

Cairo

River Nile

EGYPT

Red Sea

SUDAN

Khartoum

Blue Nile

White Nile

UGANDA

Lake Victoria

Traveling on the river

The ancient Egyptians made boats from reeds that grew beside the Nile. The wind carried them south; the river current carried them north. Today the Nile isn't as important as a means of transport but fishermen still use a flat-bottomed sailing boat called a *felucca*.

Top Facts

- The source of the Nile is Lake Victoria, near the Equator.

- Some explorers have followed it even farther south, to rivers in Rwanda and Burundi.

- The Nile gets its name from the Greek word "*neilos*," which means "river valley."

Ancient Egypt

The Ancient Egyptian civilization developed 5,000 years ago because of the Nile. The river flooded every year and left layers of rich silt on its banks. The Egyptians grew crops on this fertile land, and also fished in the river.

Did You Know?

The Nile is formed from two main rivers, the Blue Nile and the White Nile. They meet at Khartoum, the capital of Sudan.

The Guilin Hills

Guilin's scenery is the "finest under Heaven," according to one Chinese saying. For 2,000 years the lush green fields, spectacular caves, and strangely shaped mountains have inspired paintings, poems, and legends. The hills are not particularly high but they are magnificent, especially when they are reflected in the crystal-clear waters of the Li River, which runs through Guilin.

Asia

CHINA

Guilin

South China Sea

The Elephant Trunk

Elephant Trunk Hill is Guilin's most famous landmark. It looks like an elephant dipping its trunk into the Li River to drink. The water-filled cave between the elephant's trunk and legs acts like a mirror and creates amazing reflections.

Did You Know?

The name "Guilin" means "Forest of sweet osmanthus," because of the number of fragrant sweet osmanthus trees that grow there.

The Hills

The Guilin Hills are given names suggested by their features. Folded Brocade Hill is so called because its rock layers look like folded fabric. Solitary Beauty Peak got its name from a line in a poem written 1,500 years ago: "None can surpass this solitary peak in beauty."

The Reed Flute Cave

The stalactites, or icicle-shaped formations, hanging from the roof of Reed Flute Cave are a magical sight. Many suggest the shapes of animals or plants. The stalactites, like the hills, have their own legends telling weird and wonderful stories about how they got there.

Did You Know?

Buildings in Guilin are quite small by law, so that the surrounding hills look more impressive.

Mount Fuji

Mount Fuji's famous cone shape and snow-capped peak make it one of the world's most recognizable mountains. It is also sacred to the Japanese people.

A volcanic country

Mount Fuji rises 12,388 feet above Honshu, the largest of Japan's islands. It is the highest of the country's 186 volcanoes, and one of around 60 that are still active. When Mount Fuji last erupted, in 1707, ash covered the city of Tokyo 62 miles away.

Top Facts

- Around 300,000 people climb Mount Fuji every year.

- It was against the law for women to climb Mount Fuji until 1872.

JAPAN

Asia

• Mount Fuji

Pacific Ocean

Did You Know?

There is a post office at the summit of Mount Fuji. Letters posted from here carry the postmark "Japan's highest point."

The crater

The crater at the top of Mount Fuji is covered in snow for eight months of the year. Many climbers walk around the top of the crater, which is about 2,000 feet across. Mount Fuji actually consists of three separate volcanoes. These have erupted over a period of hundreds of thousands of years, changing the shape of the mountain dramatically. The mountain we see today was formed when the largest of the three volcanoes erupted around 10,000 years ago.

Did You Know?

In 2006 Shigeyoshi Sasaki set a new record by climbing Mount Fuji 121 times in one year.

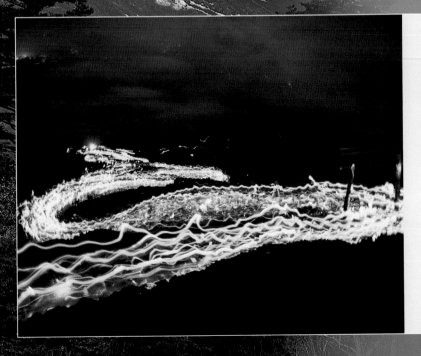

Pilgrims

Thousands of torch-carrying climbers head for the summit of Mount Fuji in time to see the spectacular sunrise. At the summit there is a shrine to the goddess Konohana-sakuya, known as the Blossom Princess. According to legend, this beautiful princess didn't want to grow old, so she rode to the top of Mount Fuji on a white horse and ascended to Heaven.

Uluru

Uluru is a sandstone mountain in the Kata Tjuta National Park in the Australian desert. The mountain is sacred to the Anangu, aboriginal people who have lived in the area for 40,000 years. They believe it played an important part in the creation of the world. Uluru rises more than 985 feet above the desert floor, but most of the sandstone is under the ground, so it is even bigger than it looks.

The sacred rock

Uluru can appear bright red or violet, depending on the weather and time of day. Anangu don't like visitors to climb Uluru because they cross a sacred "Dreamtime track." Dreamtime is when they believe the world was created.

Top Facts

- The first European people discovered Uluru in the 1900s. They called it Ayers Rock, after an Australian politician named Henry Ayers.

- The Australian government gave ownership of the rock back to the Anangu people in 1985.

- Uluru measures 5 1/2 miles all the way around the base.

Did You Know?

It is said that a piece of rock taken from Uluru as a souvenir will bring its owner bad luck.

Pacific Ocean

AUSTRALIA

Uluru

Indian Ocean

Kata Tjuta

Kata Tjuta is made up of 36 rock formations and is close to Uluru. The name "Kata Tjuta" means "many heads" in traditional Anangu language, but the rocks are often called the Olgas after the tallest peak, Mount Olga, which is about 1,800 feet high.

Soft stone

Water runs down cracks and channels in Uluru's soft sandstone surface. One Anangu legend says the cracks were made by snakelike creatures who fought a battle there.

Uluru during a thunderstorm

Yosemite

Yosemite is a vast wilderness, over 965 square miles of granite mountains, deep valleys, and spectacular waterfalls. Around 2,000 species of animals and plants live there, including Giant Sequoia trees that are almost 3,000 years old.

Yosemite
Yosemite
UNITED STATES OF AMERICA
State of California
Pacific Ocean

El Cap

Waterfalls

Yosemite is famous for its many waterfalls. Yosemite Falls are the highest in North America, at a height of 2,566 feet. The falls are best seen in spring when the amount of water flowing over them increases as the winter snow melts.

Top Facts

- Half Dome is one of Yosemite's most famous mountains. Climbers have to be careful because the mountain is often struck by lightning.

- Tourists first arrived in 1855. There were 42 that year! Today Yosemite has around four million visitors a year.

Giant Sequoias

The world's tallest, largest, and oldest trees grow in the western part of the United States. They are called Giant Sequoias. These trees are sometimes also called California redwoods because they grow in California and their wood is a reddish-brown color. Sequoias can grow to a height of 295 feet and can live for 3,000 years.

Yosemite Valley

Did You Know?

In 1864, President Abraham Lincoln passed a law to protect Yosemite's natural beauty. It became a National Park in 1890.

Bears

The black bears that roam wild in Yosemite National Park have an amazing sense of smell. Campers have to be careful as they can seek out tinned food, and will even eat soap!

The Grand Canyon

The Grand Canyon is the largest gorge on Earth. It is 5,250 feet deep, 277 miles long, and up to 18 miles wide. It was formed by the fast-flowing waters of the Colorado River, which have worn away the rock over millions of years. Wind, rain, and ice have also played a part in eroding the rock.

Layers of rock

New layers of rock are formed on the Earth's surface over millions of years, so looking at the sides of the canyon is like looking back in time. The layers at the bottom of the canyon are the oldest, formed almost two billion years ago. The top layers are quite young —just 250 million years old! Fossils buried in the layers of rock tell us about the animals that lived during different periods in the Earth's history.

Havasu Falls

Havasu Falls are famous for their blue-green color. The Havasupai tribe has lived in that area of the Grand Canyon for 800 years. The name of the tribe means "people of the bluish-green water."

The Skywalk

The Skywalk, which opened in 2007, gives an amazing view of the Grand Canyon if you don't mind heights. It juts out 65 feet over the edge and has a floor made of glass. The Colorado River is 4,000 feet below.

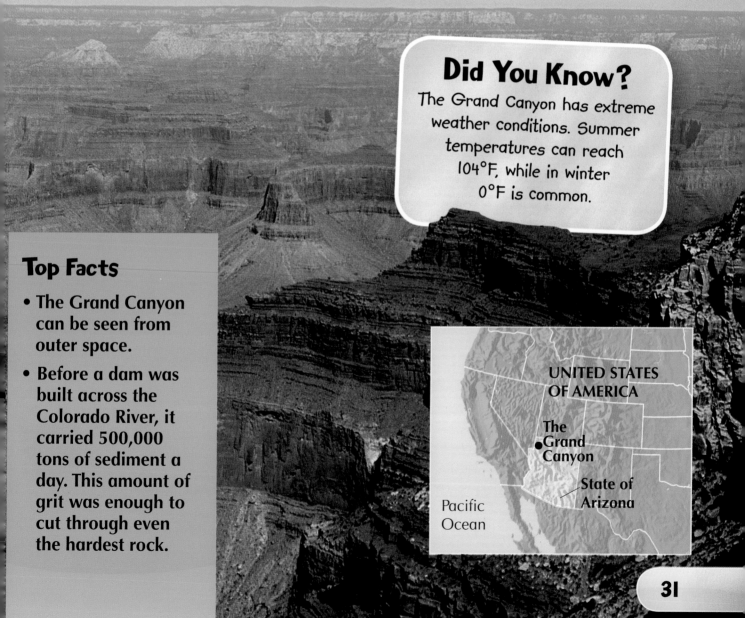

Did You Know?

The Grand Canyon has extreme weather conditions. Summer temperatures can reach 104°F, while in winter 0°F is common.

Top Facts

- The Grand Canyon can be seen from outer space.

- Before a dam was built across the Colorado River, it carried 500,000 tons of sediment a day. This amount of grit was enough to cut through even the hardest rock.

UNITED STATES OF AMERICA

The Grand Canyon

State of Arizona

Pacific Ocean

Waterfalls

Waterfalls form where a river flows over layers of hard and soft rocks lying next to each other. The water wears away the soft rock, leaving a shelf of hard rock above it. As the soft rock disappears, the waterfall gets bigger and steeper.

North
America

Niagara Falls ●

Asia

Africa

Angel Falls ●

Victoria Falls ●

South
America

Did You Know?

A daredevil acrobat called Blondin crossed Niagara Falls on a tightrope in 1859, carrying a friend on his back.

Victoria Falls

More water flows over Victoria Falls than any other waterfall in the world. These falls, which are situated in southern Africa, are 1 mile wide and 118 yards high. Over 1000 tonnes of water per second drops into the Zambezi River below. The people who live there call it "the smoke that thunders" because in the rainy season the spray, which rises hundreds of yards into the air, looks like smoke.

Top Fact

- **Waterfalls move slowly upstream. This is because the hard rock that forms the shelf eventually breaks off. Niagara Falls are moving back by 3 feet per year.**

Niagara Falls

Niagara Falls, which lie on the border between America and Canada, are among the most spectacular in the world. Water in the Niagara River has to flow around islands, so there are actually three separate waterfalls. They are called Horseshoe Falls, American Falls, and Bridal Veil Falls. At night most of Niagara's water doesn't flow over the falls. It's diverted into tunnels to turn turbines to make electricity.

Angel Falls

Angel Falls in Venezuela are the highest in the world. The water turns into a fine mist before it reaches the Churun River 1,070 yards below. Angel Falls are named after Jimmie Angel, an American adventurer who discovered them 70 years ago while searching for gold.

Victoria Falls

Did You Know?

Victoria Falls were discovered by British explorer David Livingstone in 1855. He named them after Queen Victoria, who was the British monarch at the time.

EXCITING EVENTS

We can see examples of nature's amazing beauty all around us, but nature is also powerful. In this section, we see nature revealing some of its deepest secrets, with spectacular results. Find out about winds that can toss cars around like toys, and what happens when the Earth's boiling hot core comes shooting to the surface. Discover how icebergs are formed, why some places have nights that last six months, and where to see the world's most incredible firecracker display!

Hot springs

Hot springs appear where water that is heated by molten (liquid) rock deep underground rises to the surface. The springs are often rich in minerals, because hot water dissolves minerals from the underground rocks more easily than cold water. Many people bathe in hot springs for health reasons, and sometimes the water is also used for drinking.

Bathers relax in the warm water of the Blue Lagoon at Grindavik in Iceland.

Did You Know?

Iceland uses hot water and steam from its springs to heat the country's buildings and generate nearly all the electricity it needs.

Top Facts

- Iceland has more hot springs than any other country. The average temperature of the water is 167°C.

- Hot water springs can contain 35 percent salt—that's 10 times saltier than most seas.

- The molten rock under the ground reaches temperatures as high as 1830°F.

Rotorua, New Zealand

Rotorua in New Zealand has a famous hot spring called Champagne Pool. The water is nearly 200 feet deep and has a temperature of 158°F. It is rich in minerals, including gold and silver, but it also contains sulfur. This gives the spring a yellow color—and the smell of rotten eggs!

Nagano, Japan

The hot springs at Nagano in Japan are famous for the macaque monkeys that bathe there. These monkeys began using the springs to help them survive the cold winters 40 years ago, and this behavior has passed down to their offspring.

The Northern Lights

The most spectacular light show on Earth can be seen 60 miles above the poles on dark winter nights. At the North Pole these magical displays are called the *aurora borealis*, but are commonly known as the Northern Lights.

What causes the lights?

The sun is constantly spitting out particles that fly off into space. These particles, called solar winds, collide with the Earth's magnetic field and are pushed toward the poles. The particles are electrically charged, and when they meet nitrogen and oxygen atoms in the Earth's atmosphere, it results in a dazzling show which is sometimes described as a dancing curtain of light.

Top Facts

- Solar winds travel at nearly 250 miles per second. It takes four days for them to reach the Earth, which is 93 million miles from the Sun.

- The reaction that causes the lights can disrupt electricity supplies and damage satellites.

Did You Know?

The name "aurora borealis" has Roman and Greek roots. Aurora is the Roman goddess of the dawn and boreas is the Greek word for the north wind.

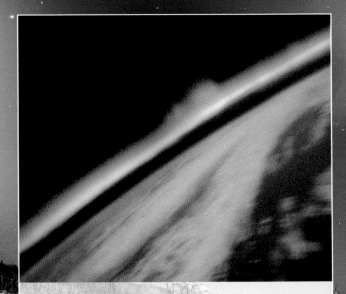

The Southern Lights

The Southern Lights, or *aurora australis*, appear around the South Pole. This picture, taken from the space shuttle *Discovery*, shows how the aurora rides above the Earth's atmosphere.

Colorful displays

The light shows are mostly green, but red, blue, or purple auroras are sometimes produced. The green color is created when the solar particles come into contact with oxygen in the Earth's atmosphere. Nitrogen in the atmosphere makes the lights red. Hydrogen and helium gases create blue and purple displays, which are more difficult to see.

The Northern Lights over Reykjavik in Iceland.

Did You Know?

The Earth's magnetic field protects us from the Sun's harmful radiation. Without it, there would be no life on the planet.

Lands of the midnight Sun

The North and South Poles have just two seasons, summer and winter, lasting six months each. The difference between these seasons is more dramatic than anywhere else on Earth. The poles have six months of daylight, followed by a six-month period when the Sun never rises.

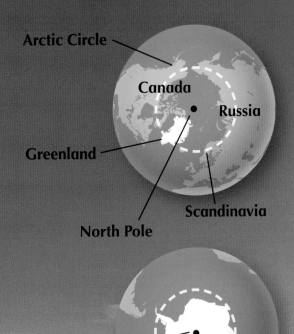

Arctic Circle

Canada

Russia

Greenland

Scandinavia

North Pole

South Pole

Antarctic Circle

evening

midnight

early morning

The midnight sun

The areas of the Earth around the poles are called the Arctic Circle in the north and the Antarctic Circle in the south. Here there are days in the middle of summer when the Sun is visible for 24 hours, the "midnight Sun," and times in the heart of winter when there is no daylight because the Sun doesn't rise. This specially created photograph shows the midnight Sun moving over Sigurdarstadavik Bay near Kopasker, Iceland. Although the Sun dips and the levels of light become lower, the Sun never disappears.

The Arctic Circle

The Antarctic Circle is not inhabited but some northerly countries such as Russia and Canada, and Scandanavian countries such as Finland and Norway, have regions that are within the Arctic Circle. Here we can see the town of Ilulissat in Greenland at 2:30 a.m. in the summer.

Glaciers

Glaciers are slow-moving rivers of ice. They are one of the most powerful forces on Earth, able to cut a path through anything in their way.

Why does a glacier form?

Glaciers are formed from layers of snow, which turn into a dense mass of ice under the pressure of their own weight. The force of gravity makes the glacier flow downhill, sometimes slicing through rock and carrying chunks along in the ice.

The largest glaciers are called ice sheets. The biggest is the Antarctica ice sheet, which covers over 5 million square miles. Although it is the coldest place on Earth, Antarctica gets just a few inches of snowfall each year. But the freezing temperatures mean that very little ice melts before the glacier reaches the sea and breaks up into icebergs.

Top Facts

- Glaciers hold 75 percent of all the world's fresh water. If they melted, the sea level would rise by almost 230 feet.

- Ten percent of the land on Earth is covered in glaciers.

Mendenhall Glacier in Alaska is about 12 miles long.

Valley glaciers

Most glaciers flow down mountainsides and through valleys. The ice scours a path through the valley, picking up rocks and boulders. These are left in a pile at the glacier's end, called the snout. Here the ice melts and forms streams and lakes.

Grey glacier in Chile, South America.

Jakobshavn Glacier

Jakobshavn Glacier in Greenland is the fastest-flowing glacier in the world, travelling at 42 feet per day. Meserve Glacier in Antarctica is a slowcoach in comparison, moving at around six feet per year. The speed at which a glacier moves doesn't just depend on how steep the slope is. Some glaciers slide along on a layer of water, which makes them flow more quickly than those that are frozen to the bedrock.

Nature in flower

Trees and plants change color dramatically as they go through their amazing life cycle. Millions of people around the world go to see the dazzling display as nature bursts into life.

Tulip fields in Holland

Holland is the world's most famous flower garden. It produces 70 percent of the world's flowers. It is best known for its tulips, which are the country's national symbol. Five hundred types of tulip are grown there, and the huge fields of flowers attract many visitors in April and May, when the tulips bloom.

Top Facts

- Holland went tulip mad in the 1600s. The demand for these flowers was so high that some rare varieties cost more than a house!

- In Japan, television reports tell the people where to go to see the best cherry blossom.

Cherry blossom time in Japan

The Japanese cherry tree, with its beautiful pink and white flowers, is sacred to the people of that country. For over 1,000 years the Japanese have celebrated the appearance of new blossom each spring in a festival called Hanami. The parties last for a week, until the blossoms begin to fall.

Desert flowers in California

In the Anza-Borrego Desert in California hundreds of plant species survive in temperatures that can reach 104°F. The desert might get its entire rainfall for the year—about 4 inches—in one storm. Some plants have deep roots to reach down for water, while others have shallow, wide roots to make the most of any rain that falls. When the rain comes the desert is transformed overnight and the ground is covered in a carpet of flowers.

Fall color in America

The forests of New England are famous for the spectacular color changes that happen each fall. The green leaves of these thick hardwood forests turn into a patchwork of red, orange, yellow, and purple. The trees stop the flow of sap to the leaves as they prepare for winter, and this causes the dramatic color change in the leaves.

Mount Etna

At 10,920 feet high, Mount Etna towers over the Italian island of Sicily. It is the highest and most active volcano in Europe. Its summit is nearly always bubbling with lava.

Europe

ITALY

Mediterranean Sea

SICILY

● Mount Etna

Why does a volcano erupt?

At the Earth's core the temperature is over 7,200°F. This extreme heat creates molten rock, called magma, which rises to the Earth's surface. An erupting volcano is this boiling liquid and gas breaking through the Earth's crust as a lava flow.

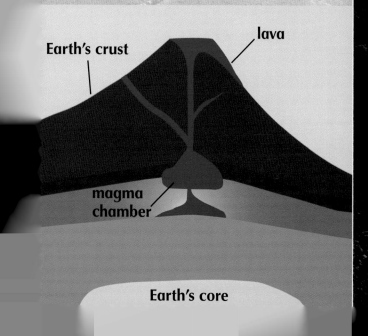

lava

Earth's crust

magma chamber

Earth's core

Lava flows

During an eruption hot, liquid rock called lava pours out of the top of the volcano and spills down the sides like bubbling syrup. The lava reaches temperatures of 1,830°F. Lava can travel very quickly, reaching 120 miles an hour when flowing down a mountainside.

The damage from ash

Ash is formed from small particles of rock that explode from the volcano. Clouds of ash are often blasted high into the Earth's atmosphere. It pollutes the air, and can kill animals and plants and damage machinery. The smallest particles of ash travel in the wind and cover vast areas of the Earth.

The Indian monsoon

For eight months of the year, India is bone dry, but in June the monsoon season begins and the country is lashed by torrential rainfall that lasts until September.

What causes monsoons?

Monsoons are caused by two geographical features that lie to the north of India. One is the Himalayan Mountains, the other is the land of Tibet, which lies just beyond the mountain range. Tibet is very flat, and in the summer the land heats up like a giant hotplate, warming the air above it. This warm air rises, and moist air from the Indian Ocean is sucked in to fill the gap. But before this damp air can reach Tibet, it strikes the Himalayan Mountains, which act like a barrier. Clouds form, and these produce huge rainstorms that last for three months.

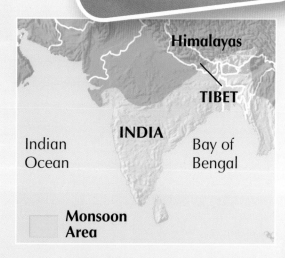

Himalayas

TIBET

INDIA

Indian Ocean

Bay of Bengal

Monsoon Area

Monsoon clouds over the city of Mumbai

Top Facts

- The word "monsoon" comes from the Arabic word "mausam" which means season.

- Monsoons affect many parts of southeast Asia, not just India. Some areas of Africa also have monsoon seasons, and parts of the southwest states of the USA are affected by monsoon-like weather.

Welcoming the monsoon

An umbrella doesn't give much protection in the monsoon season, when the rain is bouncing off the ground. The people may get a regular soaking, but the monsoon brings a welcome end to the stifling heat and humidity of India's summer months.

Floods can cause terrible damage, but the Indian people still celebrate the start of the monsoon season because it marks the end of a long period of drought. Without the monsoon rain, crops would fail and there would be famine.

A family in flooded Bihar, India, use a boat to transport food for their cattle.

Did You Know?
Cherrapunji in northeast India gets 430 inches of rain per year, making it one of the world's wettest places.

Hawaiian surf

Hawaii is the world's most isolated land, over 1,800 miles from any continent. The islands are pounded by monster waves from the surrounding Pacific Ocean, making Hawaii the surfing capital of the world.

North America

HAWAIIAN ISLANDS

South America

Pacific Ocean

Surf waves

Hawaii's huge waves are caused by storms hundreds of miles away. Winter storms off the coast of Alaska bring waves crashing onto the island's northern shores, and tropical storms in the south Pacific send big waves onto the southern beaches during the summer months. The bottom of the wave slows up when it meets the sloping seabed surrounding the islands. Meanwhile, the top of the wave plunges forward and topples over, creating perfect surfing conditions.

Top Facts

- The major surfing championships take place in Hawaii between November and February, when waves can reach nearly 50 feet high.

- A volcano called Loihi is erupting under the sea. One day it will rise up and become Hawaii's ninth island, though it may take 30,000 years!

- Hawaii became the 50th state of the United States of America in 1959.

Volcanic beaches

The jagged coastline of the volcanic Hawaiian islands is very distinctive, with large pieces of lava rock protruding out into the sea. Hawaiian beaches are often made from black sand because some of the hot lava hits the ocean and breaks into tiny pieces. Its color comes from dark minerals in the rocks.

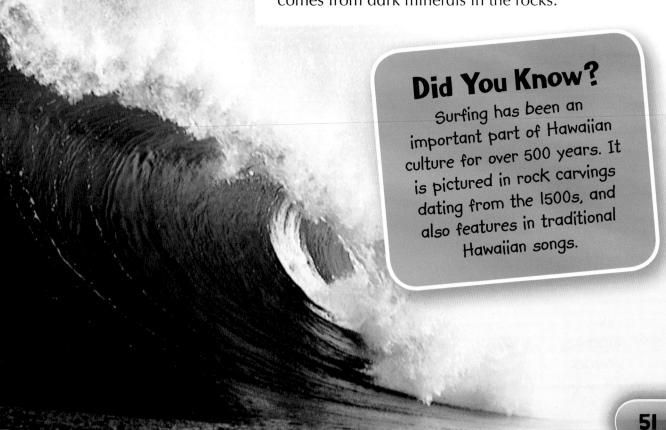

Did You Know?

Surfing has been an important part of Hawaiian culture for over 500 years. It is pictured in rock carvings dating from the 1500s, and also features in traditional Hawaiian songs.

Tornado Alley, North America

Three fourths of the world's tornadoes occur in an area called Tornado Alley in the center of the USA.

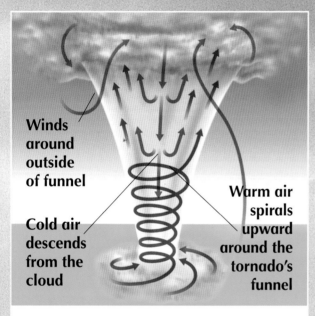

Winds around outside of funnel

Cold air descends from the cloud

Warm air spirals upward around the tornado's funnel

What is a tornado?

A tornado is a very fast, spinning wind that creates a funnel shape in the air. The winds inside can reach speeds of over 250 miles an hour.

Why do they happen so often?

In Tornado Alley the cold air from the Rocky Mountains in the north meets warm air from the southeast of the USA, forming enormous groups of clouds called "supercells." It is these supercells that cause thunderstorms and tornadoes.

Top Facts

- Tornadoes are smaller and faster than hurricanes and don't last as long, but they can still cause terrible destruction.

- In the United States there are over 700 tornadoes every year. Texas, Oklahoma, and Kansas are the worst hit states.

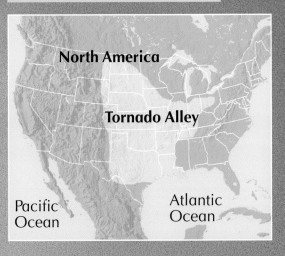

North America

Tornado Alley

Pacific Ocean

Atlantic Ocean

Storm chasers

Some people, especially scientists, like to get very close to tornadoes. These people are known as storm chasers. They take photographs and videos, often to study extreme weather conditions.

Did You Know?

Tornadoes can strike the United States of America at any time of the year, though most occur in spring and fall.

Destruction

When a tornado spins it is like an enormous vacuum cleaner sucking up air and objects from the ground. A powerful tornado can lift up cars and buildings as well as people and animals, causing a great deal of damage.

Old Faithful geyser Yellowstone Park

Old Faithful is the world's most famous geyser. It is situated in Yellowstone National Park, in the northwest of the USA. Yellowstone has over 300 geysers, more than any other place in the world.

Why do geysers spout?

Geysers are usually found where boiling hot liquid rock, called magma, lies near the Earth's surface. This is the case at Yellowstone Park, because a volcano erupted there half a million years ago, and there is still magma 3½ miles underground.

This hot rocks heats the surrounding water and the hot water rises to the Earth's surface as steam. The steam's path is blocked by cold water lying on the surface, and there is a build-up of pressure. Eventually, a fountain of hot water and steam, called a geyser, shoots into the air, and the cycle begins all over again.

Old Faithful erupts every 35 to 120 minutes, sending 8,800 gallons of water 160 feet into the sky.

Did You Know?

Old Faithful isn't the highest-spouting geyser at Yellowstone. That honor goes to Steamboat, the world's tallest active geyser, which shoots water and steam 325 feet into the air.

Old Faithful

Old Faithful was discovered in 1870, and two years later Yellowstone became the world's first national park. Today, about three million people a year visit the park to see the geysers and hot springs, and also the amazing wildlife. Yellowstone has grizzly bears, elk, bison, and wolves, while bald eagles soar high above the vast pine forests.

Top Facts

- An Old Faithful eruption can last from 1½ to 5 minutes.
- "Geyser" comes from an Icelandic word meaning "upwards force."

Did You Know?

Some of the rocks in the Earth's crust reach temperatures of 1,830°F.

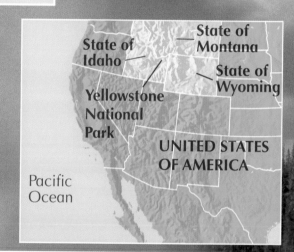

State of Idaho

State of Montana

State of Wyoming

Yellowstone National Park

UNITED STATES OF AMERICA

Pacific Ocean

Grand Prismatic Spring

Yellowstone Park has some of the world's largest hot springs, including Grand Prismatic Spring, which is 295 feet long, 246 feet wide, and 164 feet deep. The water temperature can reach 187°F in the middle of the spring. The amazing bands of color at the edges are caused by algae and bacteria.

The San Andreas Fault

The San Andreas Fault is one of the world's most famous earthquake zones. The fault is 800 miles long and runs close to some of the most populated areas in the United States.

San Andreas Fault

United States of America

San Francisco

Los Angeles

Pacific Ocean

Earthquake line

A fault line is a crack in the Earth's surface, where two of the massive plates that make up the Earth's crust meet. Sometimes the plates grind their way past each other, sometimes one plate rides up over another, creating a build-up of pressure. An earthquake occurs when the ground suddenly shifts, releasing huge amounts of energy. Earthquakes usually occur along fault lines.

The San Andreas Fault consists of four large cracks in the Earth's crust and many smaller ones. Minor tremors occur regularly along this fault line, and there have also been major earthquakes here.

Did You Know?

An earthquake occurs somewhere in the world every 30 seconds, although most of these do not cause any damage.

Top Facts

- The last earthquake to hit San Francisco was in 1989, when half a mile of road collapsed.

- Earthquakes are measured on the Richter Scale, named after the man who invented it in 1935, Charles Richter.

Moving plates

This road running across the San Andreas Fault shows the layers of rock that have been forced downwards by the pressure of the moving plates. The Pacific Plate is moving northwest past the North American Plate, at a rate of between half an inch and nearly 2 inches per year.

Did You Know?

Scientists have discovered that there are "moonquakes" —earthquakes on the Moon. While even a powerful earthquake lasts only a minute or so, a moonquake can continue for 10 minutes.

Earthquake damage

The earthquake that struck San Francisco in 1906 lasted just one minute, but caused many buildings to collapse. Broken gas pipes started fires that became an even bigger problem. The city's water pipes had also snapped during the earthquake, and the fire raged for three days before rain came to the rescue. By then, 28,000 homes had been destroyed and 700 people had lost their lives.

The turtles of Mexico

During the summer and fall months several breeds of turtle swim along the coast of Mexico. The females mate with the males and then hundreds of them crawl up onto the beaches to lay their eggs.

North America

Atlantic Ocean

Pacific Ocean

MEXICO

Rancho Nuevo

South America

Laying eggs

Turtles often return to the beach where they were born to lay their eggs. The female digs a hole and lays up to 200 eggs, which she covers with sand before returning to the sea. Covering the eggs protects them from predators, stops them from drying out in the sun, and helps them stay at a constant temperature.

Top Facts

- **The sex of a baby turtle depends on the temperature during the incubation of the egg.**

- **The eggs take about two months to hatch.**

Nests

After hatching from the egg the young turtle has to dig its way to the surface, before making its way to the sea. During this short journey many are killed by predators. On some beaches people volunteer to help the turtles reach the water safely.

Did You Know?

Sea turtles use the Earth's magnetic field to navigate their way around the ocean. This enables them to return to the place where they were born.

Rancho Nuevo

Most of the female Kemp's Ridley turtles return to one particular beach in Mexico called Rancho Nuevo. They come ashore in large groups. This arrival on the beach is known as the "arribada," meaning "arrival."

AMAZING HABITATS

It is amazing how animals and plants get used to any conditions that planet Earth can throw at them. In this section, you will learn about some extraordinary habitats, and the animal and plant species that live there. Find out which place gets more rain in an hour than some deserts get in 30 years, and where to find penguins basking under a hot tropical sun. You'll meet a flower that's bigger than a trashcan lid—and smells worse than the trash inside! You will also learn about the only living thing that can be seen from outer space.

The Arctic

The Arctic is the area surrounding the North Pole. It is a vast sheet of ice that floats on the Arctic Ocean. This ice sheet grows and shrinks, depending on the season. The Arctic Ocean, the northern parts of North America, Europe, and Russia, and almost the whole of Greenland, are within the area called the Arctic Circle.

Arctic Circle
North America
Russia
North Pole
Greenland
Europe

Adaptable animals

The Arctic fox has adapted to its environment by growing long fur that changes color with the season. Its long hair is snow-white in the winter but in summer it turns a brownish-gray color, which matches the color of the rocks in the landscape. This helps to camouflage the animal as it creeps up on its prey.

Top Facts

- Many scientists think that because of global warming, in 10 years' time the Arctic will have no ice at all during the summer months.

- The American Robert Peary claimed to be the first person to reach the North Pole, on April 6, 1909.

Baby seal

King of the Arctic

Polar bears are well suited to life in the freezing Arctic climate. They can swim in the icy Arctic Ocean without freezing as their thick oily fur coat, tough hide, and a layer of fat called blubber help to keep them warm. Polar bears also have wide feet, which act like snowshoes.

Did You Know?

Average winter temperatures in the Arctic are around -35°F, though the coldest recorded temperature is -90°F.

The walrus

The Arctic Ocean is home to many species of whales, seals, and walruses. These animals can survive in the icy waters, protected by thick layers of fat. During the winter and spring walruses spend much of their time drifting on large pieces of ice. They use their long tusks to pull themselves out of the water as well as to rake up food such as shellfish from the sea floor.

The Sahara

The Sahara is the world's largest desert, covering most of northern Africa. It is one of the hottest places on Earth, but it is the dryness of the place that makes it a desert, not its heat. Only around $2\frac{1}{2}$ inches of rain fall per year on average. Most of the desert is rocky, although there are many high sand dunes.

Pools of water

An oasis is an area in the desert where water trapped deep under the ground comes to the surface. This allows plants and trees to grow and provides small patches of green among the desert's rocks and sand. Oases are also vital water sources for people who live in the desert. People can settle here and grow crops such as date palms.

Camels—ships of the desert

Camels are used to carry goods across the Sahara, like ships carry goods across the sea. They have adapted well to life in the desert. Their humps contain fat, which can provide them with both food and water. Their wide feet allow them to walk on soft sand and they have thick soles to withstand heat from the ground. They can also close their nostrils against the sand and dust of the desert.

Desert animals

Snakes, gerbils, lizards, and scorpions all live in the desert. These small animals may hide from the hot sun in the shade of the rocks or dig burrows in the sand. The fat-tailed scorpion hides away under stones or logs. It grows up to 4 inches long and is one of the most deadly scorpions in the world.

Did You Know?

The world's highest recorded temperature in the shade was in the Sahara on September 13, 1922—a sizzling 136°F at Al Aziziyan in Libya.

Lake Nakuru

Lake Nakuru in Kenya is one of the world's most famous soda lakes. It was formed when high temperatures caused much of the water to evaporate, leaving behind salt deposits. Few animals can survive in the salty water, but flamingos have adapted well and gather at Lake Nakuru in their thousands.

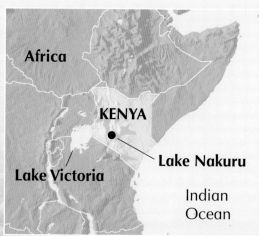

Flamingos

The flamingos that come to the lake feed on algae. Algae are tiny plants which are able to live in the warm, salty water. Flamingos are gray when they hatch but a chemical called beta carotene, which they get from their food, causes them to change color and become pink.

Did You Know?

Nakuru means "dust" or "dusty place" in the Maasai language.

Baboons

Olive baboons live in the open grassland and woodland areas surrounding Lake Nakuru. These animals eat just about anything, including insects and small mammals. They also search for grass, leaves, seeds, and fruits around the edges of the lake.

Rhinoceros

Nakuru is an important breeding place for both black and white rhinoceros. Their names are misleading as both the rhinos are actually gray in color. The word "white" comes from the Afrikaans word for "wide" and refers to the size of the white rhino's mouth.

Madagascar

Madagascar is a large island off the southeastern coast of Africa. It was cut off from the mainland more than 150 million years ago. Since then the animals and plants on Madagascar have evolved without influence from the rest of the world. Now there are thousands of species on the island that are found nowhere else on Earth.

Changing colors!

Many species of chameleon live on the island of Madagascar. Chameleons are known for their ability to change color, and many people believe that chameleons change color to match their surroundings. In fact their skin changes in response to temperature, light, and mood.

Madagascan frogs

The tomato frog is just one of many strange kinds of frog that live in the shallow pools and swamps in the lowlands of Madagascar. The male frog is smaller and is not as brightly colored as the female. The tomato frog releases a sticky glue-like liquid through its skin that protects it against snakes and other creatures.

Top Facts

• The rosy periwinkle, a plant which lives only in Madagascar, is used by doctors to treat cancer.

• Frogs are the only amphibians found on Madagascar—there are no toads, newts, or salamanders.

Many different kinds of baobab trees grow on Madagascar.

Did You Know?

The lemurs of Madagascar are an endangered species because the forests where they live are being destroyed.

Indian Ocean

Africa

MADAGASCAR

Lemurs

Madagascar is the only place on Earth where lemurs can be found. Lemurs look a bit like monkeys as they have grasping fingers and toes and forward-looking eyes. But there are differences because the lemur has large, round eyes and a snout that looks as though it could belong to a cat or dog!

The Serengeti

The word "Serengeti" comes from the Maasai language and means "endless plains" or "extended place." The Serengeti is a vast area of grassland or savannah spanning over 18,600 miles, in Tanzania, East Africa.

The great migration

Wildebeests, gazelles, and zebra are the animals most commonly found in this area. They take part in the yearly Serengeti migration, which is one of the great wonders of the natural world. Nearly two million animals follow a circular route around the plains of East Africa, covering nearly 800 miles, in search of water.

Top Facts

- Elephants are the largest, heaviest land animals, and the second tallest, after the giraffe. An African male elephant—called a bull—can weigh as much as six cars.

- Zebras can sense a rainstorm from 60 miles away. They are first to reach the lush grass that the rain brings, while wildebeest and gazelles follow on behind.

Hunters

The grasslands and plains provide food and shelter for large hunting animals including lions, cheetahs, and hyenas. Lions are skillful hunters, usually working in groups to improve their chances of success. Their eyes are adapted for seeing at night, when they go out searching for prey on the savannah.

A lioness with her cub

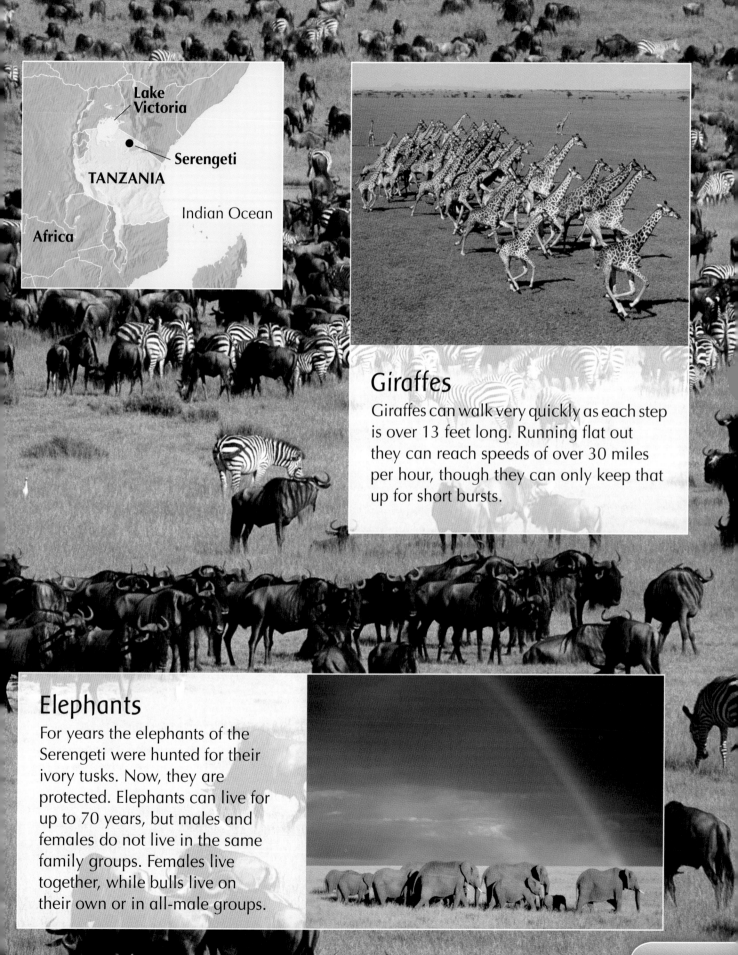

Lake
Victoria

Serengeti

TANZANIA

Indian Ocean

Africa

Giraffes

Giraffes can walk very quickly as each step is over 13 feet long. Running flat out they can reach speeds of over 30 miles per hour, though they can only keep that up for short bursts.

Elephants

For years the elephants of the Serengeti were hunted for their ivory tusks. Now, they are protected. Elephants can live for up to 70 years, but males and females do not live in the same family groups. Females live together, while bulls live on their own or in all-male groups.

Sichuan, China

China's remote mountain regions are home to some of the world's rarest animals. Many of them now live in nature reserves, which have been created to protect them and their habitats.

The giant panda

The panda is a member of the bear family and classed as a carnivore, or meat eater, but the leaves and shoots of the bamboo plant form 99 percent of the panda's diet. Bamboo gives them little nourishment, so they make up for it by eating vast amounts, up to 28 pounds each day. China is the only place where the giant panda lives in the wild. The giant panda is an endangered species but the numbers are rising slowly as they are protected in nature reserves and are also bred in captivity to be released into the wild.

Top Facts

- Giant panda babies are tiny. They weigh less than a large apple when born.

- Giant pandas don't hibernate when the weather gets cold. Instead they move farther down the mountain, where it is warmer.

Red pandas

The red panda also feeds mainly on bamboo and can eat almost half its body weight every day. It sleeps in the trees during the day, as this diet only provides enough energy for eating and resting.

CHINA   Sichuan

Asia

Indian Ocean

Monkeys

An adult golden snub-nosed monkey protects its cub from predators, which include hawks, wolves, and tigers. The golden snub-nosed monkey gets its name from the orange fur on its face and its flattened nose. Its body fur grows up to 6 inches long as this monkey has to cope with the coldest temperatures of any ape species, down to -17°F.

The Sumatran rain forest

The Indonesian island of Sumatra in Southeast Asia has one of the largest areas of tropical rain forests in the world. Tropical rain forests are found near the Equator. It is warm and wet there every single day, so plants grow all year round.

Asia

Sumatra

INDONESIA

Indian Ocean

Endangered tigers

The beautiful Sumatran tiger is one of the world's most endangered species. Experts think there are fewer than 500 left. Tigers and other species are under threat because of hunting and the destruction of their habitat by farmers, who clear trees to grow crops or cut them down to sell the wood.

Top Fact

• Rain forests cover only 6 percent of the Earth's surface, but over half of all the animal and plant species live there.

• Rain forests get at least 6 feet of rainfall every year, and the average temperature is around 77°F.

Orangutans

The word "orangutan" means "man of the forest" in the local language. Orangutans spend most of their lives in the trees, where they climb slowly and carefully, searching for wild figs, leaves, and insects. Orangutans have large hands and feet, which have a powerful grip. Just one hand or foot on a branch can carry the ape's entire weight. Orangutans often hang upside down to eat. They build nests in the trees where the females and young males sleep at night. The heavier males sleep on the forest floor. The young orangutans stay with their mothers for up to six years.

Did You Know?

The Titum Arum is a spiky flower that grows up to about 9 feet tall in the Sumatran rain forest. It can take seven years for this plant to flower, then it dies a few days later!

Huge flowers

The largest single flower in the world, giant rafflesia, grows in Sumatra. It can reach up to 3 feet across. Its powerful smell of rotting meat attracts flies, which then carry the plant's pollen from one flower to another.

The Great Barrier Reef

The Great Barrier Reef is the largest living thing in the world. It is formed from millions of tiny animals called coral polyps, which have joined together to form a reef that runs for 1,240 miles along the northeast coast of Australia.

Indian Ocean

The Great Barrier Reef

AUSTRALIA

Indian Ocean

A clown fish on the reef

What is coral?

Coral polyps are tiny sea creatures with limestone shells. Over the centuries these shells build up to form coral reefs. Although corals are animals, they need sunlight to grow, like plants. That's because the corals contain thousands of tiny plants called algae. Like all plants, the algae use sunlight to make food, both for themselves and for the coral. It is the algae that give the coral its bright colors.

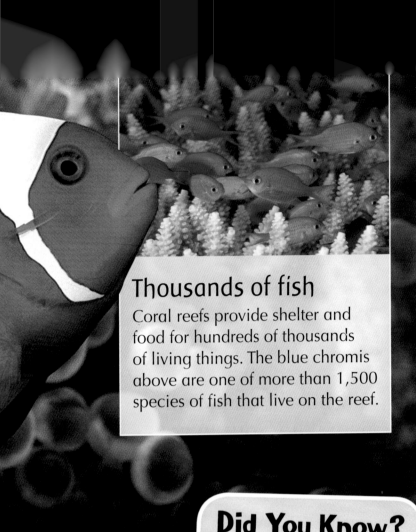

Thousands of fish

Coral reefs provide shelter and food for hundreds of thousands of living things. The blue chromis above are one of more than 1,500 species of fish that live on the reef.

Turtles

Six species of sea turtle are found in the waters around the Great Barrier Reef. Turtles, like this green turtle, spend most of their lives in the ocean, feeding on sea grasses and corals, though females come ashore to lay their eggs.

Did You Know?

The Great Barrier Reef is the only living thing that can be seen from space.

Top Fact

• The reef is under threat from rising sea temperatures. The warm water stops the algae inside the coral from producing food. The algae become poisonous, so the coral spits them out. Without the algae to provide food, the coral dies and turns white.

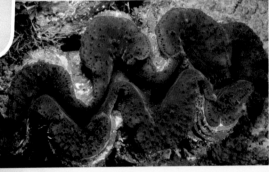

Giant clams

The shell of a giant clam can measure up to 47 inches in length and weigh nearly 500 pounds. Once a clam fastens itself to a spot on a reef, it stays there for the rest of its life.

The Rocky Mountains

The Rocky Mountains form the backbone of North America. They stretch from Alaska, through the western parts of Canada and the USA, coming to an end in New Mexico. The tallest mountains are over 157,000 feet high with jagged, rocky peaks and slopes covered in snow and glaciers. Others have gentle slopes with rounded tops.

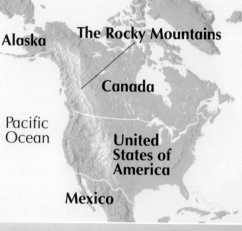

Alaska

The Rocky Mountains

Canada

Pacific Ocean

United States of America

Mexico

Mountain animals

Deer, elk, and coyotes are some of the larger mammals found in the Rockies, but mountain lions are the most magnificent. The mountain lion, sometimes known as the cougar, is a solitary animal that hunts by day and night. It will eat just about anything—from a grasshopper to a deer.

Keeping warm

Winters in the Rocky Mountains can be bitterly cold with deep snow and high winds. Black, brown, and grizzly bears are protected in these cold winter months by their thick fur coats and layer of fat. In summer and early fall they eat plenty of fruits, nuts, and berries as well as insects, roots, and small mammals in order to build up their store of fat for the winter.

Top Facts

- Early explorers gave the mountains their name because of the rugged landscape.

- The highest peak in the Rocky Mountains is Mount Elbert in Colorado, at 14,435 feet.

Mountain goat

The mountain goat is a sturdy animal, with a coat made of thick, coarse hair, to protect it from the cold and fierce winds. Its hooves have a hard outside rim and cushioned inner pad, which help it to bound over rocks.

The Everglades

The Everglades is a vast wilderness of swamp and marshland in southern Florida. The shallow waters and 10,000 islands are home to some rare and endangered species, such as the enormous manatee.

UNITED STATES OF AMERICA

Florida

Atlantic Ocean

Gulf of Mexico

The ● Everglades

What grows in the Everglades?

Much of the land in the Everglades is covered with sawgrass, which grows to a height of 9 to 15 feet. Sawgrass is very sharp. It has tiny teeth along the edges of the blades that can cut flesh. There are many hummocks, or small, fertile, raised areas, on which palms, pine trees, cypresses, and other trees and shrubs can grow.

Did You Know?

There are four species of poisonous snake in the Everglades. These are the cottonmouth, the diamondback rattlesnake, the dusky pygmy rattlesnake, and the coral snake.

Roots

Where the swamps border the coastline, the trees have adapted to live in salt water. Their roots stick out of the mud to help the plants take in oxygen they need from the air.

The gentle manatee

The Everglades are home to the manatee in the winter months. Manatees are marine mammals and they are forced to come to the surface to breathe air. Like seals, they have blubber under their thick skin to protect them from the cold and can weigh up to 990 pounds. The manatee feeds on the sea grasses and plants that grow in the shallow water of the Everglades.

Alligators

The alligator is one of over 50 species of reptile that live in the Everglades. Alligators are fierce predators, but they also play an important part in the survival of many species. During the dry winter months, from December to April, alligators dig large holes where water collects. This helps insects, turtles, fish, and wading birds to survive until the rainy season arrives—but they have to try to avoid being eaten by the alligators!

The Amazon rain forest

The Amazon rain forest is the largest in the world, covering over two million square miles, an area around the size of Australia. It is home to more plant and animal species than any other habitat on Earth, and new ones are being discovered every year.

The Amazon River

The Amazon River flows over 4,000 miles from the Andes Mountains in Peru to the Atlantic Ocean. The Amazon and the 1,000 smaller rivers that feed into it hold 20 percent of all the world's fresh water. Over 3,000 gallons of water flow from the Amazon into the Atlantic Ocean every second. The seawater is diluted so much by the fresh water from the Amazon that it is still only slightly salty 90 miles out into the ocean.

The forest floor

Jaguars are the Amazon rain forest's fiercest hunters. Their spotted coat helps to keep them hidden in the undergrowth as they stalk their prey, which includes cattle and pigs. The rain forest floor is dark because most of the sunlight is absorbed in the treetops 130 feet above. The branches spread out to form a large leafy blanket called a canopy, where most of the rain forest's plants and animals live.

Colorful birds

Macaws are one of 1,500 bird species that live in the rain forest. These brightly colored members of the parrot family gather in large numbers on the clay cliffs of the Amazon River. Here they feed on minerals that are thought to protect them from any poisons in the seeds they eat. Macaws use their powerful hooked beaks to crack open the shells that surround the seeds.

Did You Know?

More than 2 inches of rain can fall in an hour in the Amazon rain forest. The rain forest canopy is so thick that after heavy rainfall it can take 10 minutes for the first drops of water to reach the forest floor.

The anaconda

The anaconda is the world's largest snake, able to grow to over 32 feet long. It is an excellent swimmer and climber and is usually found along the river's edge, waiting for an unlucky creature to come to the bank to drink. This powerful snake will attack animals as large as deer and goats. It kills its prey by coiling around it and squeezing tightly, or by dragging it under water and drowning it.

The Galapagos Islands

The Galapagos Islands, which lie 620 miles off the west coast of South America, provide some amazing sights that can't be seen anywhere else in the world. There are iguanas basking in the sun and tortoises strong enough to carry a man.

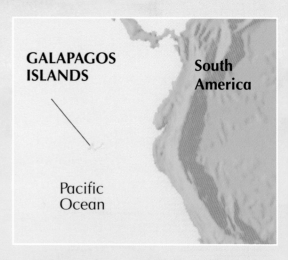

GALAPAGOS ISLANDS

South America

Pacific Ocean

Volcanic islands

The Galapagos Islands were originally formed by volcanoes, some of which are still active. There is a huge variety of habitats, including sandy beaches, rocky cliffs, and deserts. Over the centuries, animals and plants have adapted to the different island habitats. This means that the same species can look quite different, depending on which island it is from.

Giant tortoise

In the 1500s Spanish explorers named the islands after their most amazing inhabitant, the giant tortoise. "Galapago" means tortoise in Spanish. These creatures can weigh up to 550 pounds and live for over 100 years. Local people can tell which island a tortoise is from by the shape of its shell.

Strange creatures!

Galapagos is the only place in the world where sea-going iguanas are found. After swimming in the sea, these cold-blooded reptiles warm themselves by sunbathing on the hot black volcanic rocks at the edge of the water. Giant land iguanas, which are 3 feet or more in length, live farther inland.

Bird life

There are very few species of birds on the Galapagos but some of them are quite unusual. There are cormorants that are such fantastic swimmers that, over time, they have lost the ability to fly, and penguins that bask in the sunshine. One of the most interesting birds is the blue-footed booby, which performs a dance, flapping its bright blue feet, when it wants to attract a mate.

ANCIENT WONDERS

Some of the world's most amazing structures were built long before the wheel was invented, never mind cranes and trucks! Transporting yourself 250 miles was hard enough 4,000 years ago, so imagine what it was like moving stones weighing 4 tons that distance. In this section, you will find out where that happened, and discover many other wonders of the ancient world, such as the stadium where Roman gladiators and wild beasts fought to the death, and cave paintings that are 16,000 years old.

Stonehenge

Stonehenge, in Wiltshire, England, is the most famous stone circle in the world. No one is quite sure how or why it was built—some people think it might have been a giant calendar.

Atlantic Ocean

UNITED KINGDOM

South Wales

•Stonehenge

Europe

lintel

sarsen stone

The monument

Archaeologists think Stonehenge was built in three phases over a period of time beginning in around 3,000 B.C. The original part of the structure was a large circular ditch and bank called a henge. The famous standing stones were added over a period of almost 200 years. The 82 bluestones were brought to the site first. Many people believe that they were dragged and carried on rafts from quarries in South Wales, over 200 miles away. The largest stones, called sarsen stones, were the final addition. These were placed in pairs, each pair supporting a massive horizontal lintel.

Top Facts

- **The tallest archway at Stonehenge stands 25 feet high.**

- **The bluestones are so called because they turn blue when they are wet.**

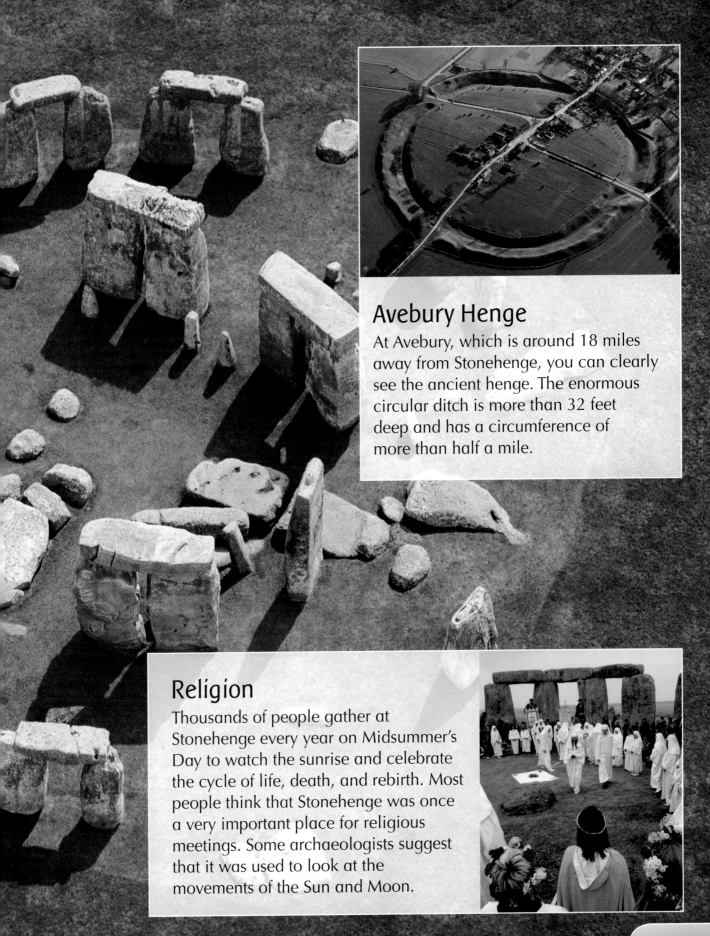

Avebury Henge

At Avebury, which is around 18 miles away from Stonehenge, you can clearly see the ancient henge. The enormous circular ditch is more than 32 feet deep and has a circumference of more than half a mile.

Religion

Thousands of people gather at Stonehenge every year on Midsummer's Day to watch the sunrise and celebrate the cycle of life, death, and rebirth. Most people think that Stonehenge was once a very important place for religious meetings. Some archaeologists suggest that it was used to look at the movements of the Sun and Moon.

Lascaux Caves

In 1940, four teenage boys followed their dog into some caves at Lascaux in southwestern France. On the walls inside they found some of the oldest paintings in the world, believed to date back at least 15,000 years.

Inside the caves

Prehistoric hunters painted the walls of the Lascaux caves. There are hundreds of paintings, many of which are deep inside the caves and difficult to reach. They show several different animals including horses, stags, cattle, bison, and even a few birds. Strangely, there are no images of reindeer, even though they were the main animals hunted by the cavemen. The pictures are in shades of red, brown, yellow, and black.

Did You Know?

The paint used in the caves was made from ground-up earth and rocks, probably mixed with animal blood and fat.

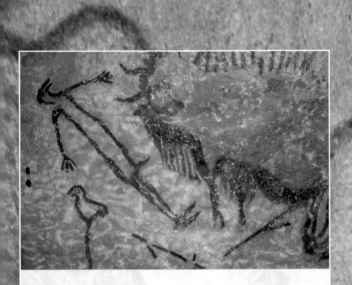

The dead man

There is only one picture of a person in the caves. The man is lying dead or dying in front of a wounded bison. It looks as though it is a painting of a hunting accident.

Why were they painted?

No one is quite sure why the hunters painted animals on the walls of caves. Some experts think that the paintings were a form of magic to help the hunters catch their prey. Another idea is that the cavemen believed that they had to paint the animals on the wall to replace those that had been killed.

The Colosseum

Plays, mock sea battles, and gladiator fights were all staged at the Colosseum during Roman times. Crowds of 50,000 packed into this huge, open-air amphitheater to see these spectacular and often bloodthirsty forms of entertainment.

Europe

ITALY

● **Rome**

Mediterranean Sea

Did You Know?

There was a tunnel underneath the Colosseum for the Emperor. It went under the seats and led straight to the royal box. This meant that he did not have to walk through the crowds to take his seat.

Gladiators

Most gladiators were slaves or criminals. They were brought to Rome from all parts of the empire and trained in special schools so that they could entertain the Colosseum crowds with bloody combat games. Gladiators were made to fight each other, or against wild beasts such as lions, tigers, and crocodiles.

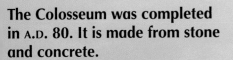

The Colosseum was completed in A.D. 80. It is made from stone and concrete.

The arena

In the center of the Colosseum there was a flat area called the arena. This is where all the action took place. Underneath the arena was a series of underground tunnels and rooms, which we can see today because the arena floor has not survived. Fighters waited here, but it was also where animals were kept for the wild beast games.

Pompeii

On August 24, A.D. 79 the volcano Vesuvius erupted with terrible results. The ash and rock that were hurled from the volcano completely buried the Roman city of Pompeii.

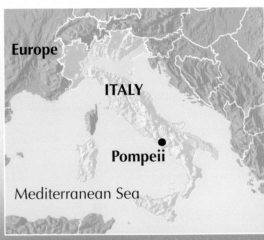

Europe

ITALY

Pompeii

Mediterranean Sea

Vesuvius

The town

Pompeii was a rich and busy town where around 20,000 people lived when the volcano erupted. Today you can walk down the streets and see the houses, shops, and temples that these Romans used. This colorful mosaic is on the wall of one of the houses.

Herculaneum Gate

Vesuvius Gate

Capua Gate

Nola Gate

Sarno Gate

Marina Gate

Stabian Gate

Nucerian Gate

Buildings
Unexcavated Areas

A large part of Pompeii is still covered by earth and has not yet been uncovered, or excavated, by archaeologists.

The ruins of Pompeii

Deadly night!

Many people who lived in Pompeii managed to escape, but some chose to shelter in their houses. When archaeologists began to explore, they found many holes. These once contained the bodies of the people and animals buried beneath the hot ash. The ash eventually turned to stone, and when the bodies decayed a hole the shape of the body was left. Lifelike casts of the victims were made by filling these holes with plaster.

Pompeii rediscovered

After the disaster, Pompeii was abandoned and forgotten. In 1748, after the city was rediscovered, archaeologists began to dig. The deep blanket of volcanic ash that covered Pompeii had helped to preserve and protect many of the buildings with their wonderful mosaics and wall paintings. This wall painting is from the Villa of the Mysteries.

The Acropolis

The Acropolis was built 2,500 years ago to protect the citizens of Athens from invaders. It stands on a hill overlooking the city, which was the safest place for the people and their sacred temples.

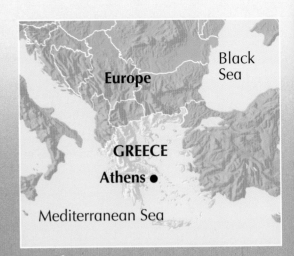

The Parthenon

The Parthenon

The Parthenon is the most famous of all the buildings on the Acropolis. It is a great temple built by the Ancient Athenians to honor Athena, the goddess of wisdom and war. The temple was built around 2,500 years ago by the command of the leader Pericles of Athens. The Ancient Greeks believed that Athena could protect their city and so they loved and worshiped her.

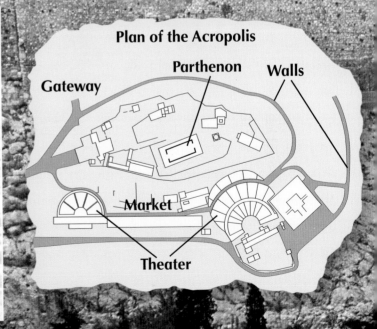

Plan of the Acropolis

The theater

The theater of Herodes Atticus was one of two open-air theaters on the Acropolis. A large semicircle of seats was cut into a hillside with a flat stage area at the bottom. Theaters were so well designed that you could hear the actors speaking on stage in the top row of seats. Those in the back rows needed help to see what was happening on stage and so actors wore masks to show who they were playing.

Greek columns

The tall, slim columns of the Parthenon and other temples were decorated with grooves, which were carved in them from top to bottom. Although the columns look perfectly straight, they actually have a bulge in the middle. This is because tall straight columns look narrower in the middle. The Greek architects did not want their columns to appear uneven and so they made them fatter in the middle.

Did You Know?

The Parthenon looks almost white today but it was originally brightly painted and decorated with many sculptures.

Knossos

Minoan kings ruled the eastern Mediterranean from Knossos, on the island of Crete, for 1,500 years. This ancient civilization, which died out around 1450 B.C., gave us many famous legends.

This courtyard was restored by the archaeologist Sir Arthur Evans.

The palace

The palace at Knossos had over 1,000 rooms connected by a maze of corridors. Legend says that the ruler, King Minos, ordered the architect Daedalus to design an even bigger maze beneath the palace. This was called the Labyrinth, and housed the Minotaur, a fearsome creature that was half man and half bull. The king disapproved when his daughter, Ariadne, fell in love with an Athenian prince called Theseus, and had him thrown into the Labyrinth. But Theseus killed the Minotaur and escaped by following a trail of string.

Did You Know?

The palace had running water and a sewage system. The water was carried in pipes made of clay.

Paintings

The walls throughout the palace were decorated with beautiful scenes from nature showing animals, plants, and sea life. The wall painting of dolphins in the Queen's Chamber is very detailed and shows their flat noses and alert eyes. They are shown swimming among small fish and seaweed.

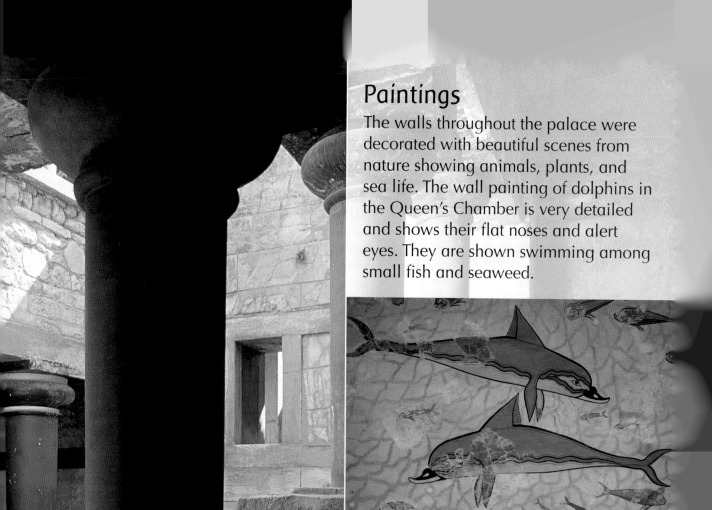

The bull dance

The wall painting of the bull-jumping is one of the most famous attractions at Knossos. No one knows whether this activity really took place but if so, it must have been a test of bravery and skill. Both young men and women are shown trying to catch hold of a bull's horns so that they can leap over its back.

The Pyramids at Giza

The pyramids are the most famous monuments of Ancient Egypt. The largest pyramid of all is the Great Pyramid at Giza, just outside the modern city of Cairo. It was built for King Khufu in around 2,528 B.C. There are two other large pyramids at Giza, which belong to Khufu's son, Khafre, and his grandson, Menkaure.

Did You Know

No one knows how the pyramids were constructed but the builders were very accurate. The base of the great pyramid is almost a perfect square.

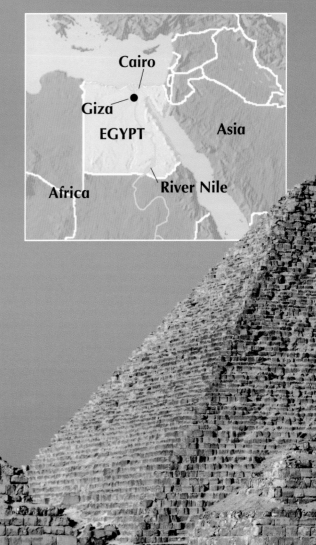

Cairo

Giza

EGYPT

Asia

Africa

River Nile

Building blocks

Khufu's Great Pyramid was built from over two million large blocks of stone cut from nearby quarries. These are believed to weigh around 2¹/₂ tons—although the stones at the base of the pyramid are even heavier. When it was originally built, the pyramid was covered with limestone blocks so that its outer surface was smooth and white.

The Sphinx

The Sphinx at Giza was carved around 4,500 years ago for the pharaoh Khafre. It guarded the way to his pyramid. The Sphinx is carved from limestone and has the head of the king combined with the body of a lion, making a link between the strength of the lion and the pharaoh's great power.

Did You Know?

Although the pyramids are believed to have been the burial places of the pharaohs, no one has ever found the mummy of a pharaoh in a pyramid.

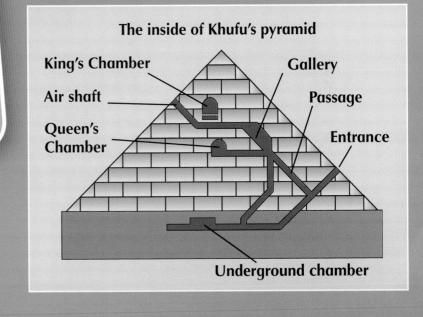

The inside of Khufu's pyramid

King's Chamber

Air shaft

Queen's Chamber

Gallery

Passage

Entrance

Underground chamber

The Temples at Karnak

The Ancient Egyptian temples at Karnak, the largest group of temples ever built, are on the east bank of the River Nile just outside the modern town of Luxor.

The temples

The oldest temples at Karnak were built 4,000 years ago. More temples were added over a period of 1,600 years, under the reign of around 30 different pharaohs. The temple devoted to the god Amun-Re is the largest. A long row of sphinxes with ram's heads leads up to the enormous gate, called a pylon, of the Temple of Amun-Re.

Pylon

EGYPT — Karnak

Asia

Africa

River Nile

Carvings

The walls of the temples are covered in carvings of the pharaohs and the gods. This carving shows the pharaoh Tuthmosis III making an offering to the gods.

The hall of columns

One of the most impressive parts of the temple is the huge hall containing 134 massive columns. The columns are covered in carvings and the 12 central pillars are over 69 feet high—more than 10 times the height of an average man. This is called the Hypostyle Hall.

Hypostyle Hall

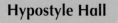

Sacred Lake

Did You Know?
The temple site covers 1.2 million square yards —that's enough space for 200 soccer pitches!

Petra

Petra has been called the "rose-red city half as old as time." The ancient city lies in a huge valley in Jordan around 50 miles south of the Dead Sea near the small town of Wadi Musa.

The rose-red city

Petra was the capital city of the Nabataeans, an Arab people who traded in silk and spices. The vast city is carved into the steep rockface on the mountainside. It is surrounded by high hills of rust-colored sandstone, which gave the city some natural protection against invaders and helped the people to control the important trading routes.

The Siq

The entrance to the city is through the Siq, a narrow winding gorge over half a mile long. The walls rise up hundreds of feet on each side.

The treasury, called Al-Khazneh

Mosaics

Petra Church is paved with some beautiful mosaics, showing many birds, animals, and landscape scenes. This mosaic shows a boy fishing.

The monastery

The monastery, called El-Deir, was built high up on the mountainside. Its name suggests that monks once lived there, but the monastery was probably a temple, dedicated to a king who was made into a god after his death. The building is 164 feet wide and two stories high. It is topped by a magnificent urn.

Dead Sea

Israel

JORDAN

Asia

● Petra

Did You Know?

The impressive front of Al-Khazneh was used in the final moments of the movie Indiana Jones and the Last Crusade.

Persepolis

Two thousand five hundred years ago the Persian Empire grew to become the most powerful on Earth. Persian emperors ruled from modern Iran, and their empire stretched from Egypt to India.

A new Persian city

In 522 B.C. the Persian emperor, Darius I, gave orders for a new capital city to be built, from where he would rule the mighty empire. It was called Persepolis, "the city of the Persians." He also began work on a magnificent royal palace, which was built on a platform 33 feet above the surrounding land.

Magnificent sculptures

This sculpture of a griffin, a mythical beast with two heads, would have been on top of one of the pillars holding up the roof of a grand hall called the Apadana. This is where the king received visitors.

The Battle of Marathon

A carving of Darius I. Darius tried to invade Greece several times, but after his fleet of ships was destroyed by a storm, his army was defeated by Greek soldiers at the famous Battle of Marathon. After the battle it was said that a messenger named Pheidippides ran the 26 miles to Athens with news of the Greek victory. In honor of Pheidippides, the 26-mile marathon became part of the first modern Olympic Games in 1896.

Darius's staircase

The stairs leading to the Apadana were decorated with many carvings. These show leaders from all parts of the empire, recognizable because of their different costumes and offerings, bringing gifts to the emperor, Darius I. The figures are carved so that they appear to be climbing the stairs.

Did You Know?

Persepolis was destroyed by fire when it was occupied by the Greek King Alexander the Great in 330 B.C.

Borobudur

Borobudur in Indonesia is the world's largest Buddhist monument. It was built around A.D. 800 but was mysteriously abandoned around 100 years later. Some people think a nearby volcano erupted, as Borobudur lay hidden beneath ash and jungle growth for almost 1,000 years.

One of the 72 statues of Buddha

What does the building mean?

Borobudur's design represents the Buddhist view of the universe. There are three levels: square terraces at the bottom, then circular ones, and the bell-shaped top. Walking up the monument is a symbol of rising up to nirvana, the Buddhist heaven. To reach nirvana Buddhists have to free themselves of all their worldly ideas and feelings, such as greed and envy.

Asia

INDONESIA

Indian Ocean

Borobudur

Did You Know?

As pilgrims walk round the six square and three circular terraces, they pass over 2,500 carvings. These show the life and teachings of Buddha and also scenes of daily life at the time the monument was built.

Bell-shaped top

Three circular levels

Square levels

Top Facts

- Over a million stone blocks were used to construct Borobudur.
- Buddhist pilgrims approach the monument from the east and walk round it in a clockwise direction.
- A structure such as Borobudur that represents the Buddhist universe is called a mandala.

Stupas

These dome-shaped shrines are called stupas. There are 72 of them, each containing a statue of Buddha. At first glance the statues all look the same, but the position of the hands varies. Different hand gestures have different meanings. For example, a raised palm stands for fearlessness. These hand gestures are called mudras.

Teotihuacán

Fifteen hundred years ago Teotihuacán in Mexico was the greatest city in North or South America, and one of the largest in the world. This ancient civilization, with a population of over 100,000, mysteriously died out around the 700s, leaving behind a number of amazing pyramid temples.

North America

Atlantic Ocean

MEXICO

●Teotihuacán

Pacific Ocean

South America

The Pyramid of the Sun is around 700 feet long and just over 200 feet high.

Quetzalcoatl's temple

The temple of the ancient god Quetzalcoatl is inside the Citadel, a large open space at the center of Teotihuacán. When archaeologists uncovered the temple in around 1920 much of it had collapsed. One side has survived and huge serpent heads made of stone, each of which weighs over 4 tons, stick out of the wall.

Sacrifices

Human sacrifices were made as gifts to the gods. Sacrifices took place on top of the temple when the priests cut out the hearts of their victims. Many groups of human skeletons have been found at Teotihuacán. Those discovered at the Temple of Quetzalcoatl seemed to be warriors, judging by their clothing. Several wore necklaces of shells carved to look like jaws with teeth.

Top Facts

• The pyramids look very plain today but when they were built they would have been decorated with colorful paintings.

• The base of the Pyramid of the Sun at Teotihuacán is as large as the base of the Great Pyramid at Giza in Egypt.

Did You Know?

Teotihuacán was built around the Avenue of the Dead, the city's main street, which runs in a north–south direction. The people believed that north represented death and the underworld, so tombs were usually built there.

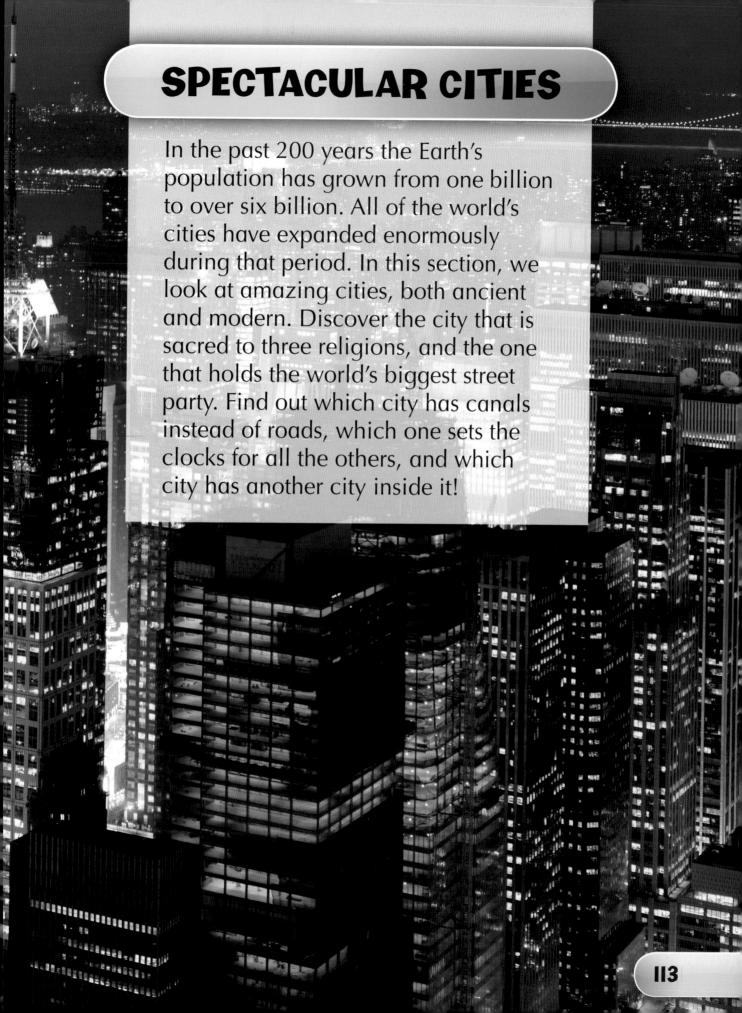

SPECTACULAR CITIES

In the past 200 years the Earth's population has grown from one billion to over six billion. All of the world's cities have expanded enormously during that period. In this section, we look at amazing cities, both ancient and modern. Discover the city that is sacred to three religions, and the one that holds the world's biggest street party. Find out which city has canals instead of roads, which one sets the clocks for all the others, and which city has another city inside it!

London

A famous writer called Samuel Johnson once said, "When a man is tired of London, he is tired of life." He meant that there is so much to see and do in the city, it is impossible to be bored. Johnson wrote that over 200 years ago, and today London has even more places of interest.

Top Facts

- Clocks all around the world are set by what time it is in a part of London called Greenwich.

- London has the world's oldest underground railroad. The first line was opened in 1863.

City on the Thames

London is centered on the River Thames. Some of the city's best-known buildings are found along its banks. The Tower of London is an ancient fortress, which was founded by William the Conqueror almost 1,000 years ago. Over the centuries the Tower has been used as a palace, a prison, and an armory. Today many people visit the Tower to see the priceless Crown Jewels, which have been kept in the tower since 1303.

Changing the Guard

Buckingham Palace is the home of the Queen and it is protected by the Household Guard, who usually wear red tunics and tall hats called bearskins. The Changing of the Guard is a colorful ceremony that takes place in front of the Palace on most mornings.

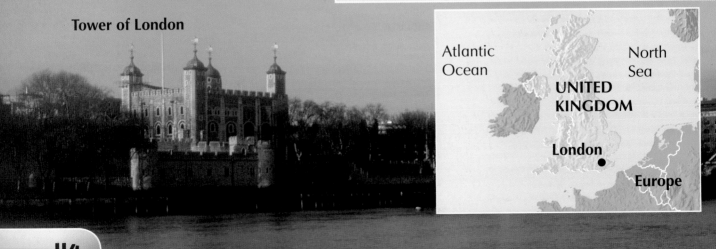

Tower of London

Atlantic Ocean

North Sea

UNITED KINGDOM

London

Europe

London Eye

The London Eye, at 443 feet high, is one of the world's largest observation wheels. During the 30-minute round trip passengers can see up to 25 miles away.

Big Ben

Big Ben is the name of the huge 14-ton bell inside the clock tower of the Houses of Parliament. It is named after Sir Benjamin Hall, the man in charge of the building when the bell was installed in 1858.

Tower Bridge was built in 1894.

Did You Know?
Thirteen million people live in London and its suburbs, making it Europe's largest city.

Paris

Paris is famous for food and fashion. It is also celebrated for its museums and galleries, and is often described as the most romantic city in the world.

River Seine

Paris is divided in two by the River Seine. The south side of the river is called the Left Bank and the north side is called the Right Bank. The Left Bank was traditionally the home of artists, writers, and philosophers. There are two natural islands in the middle of the river, the Ile de la Cité and the Ile St. Louis.

The Louvre

The Louvre was a royal palace before becoming a museum in 1793. Visitors enter the world-famous building through a 65-foot-high glass pyramid, which was added in 1993.

The Arc de Triomphe

The Arc de Triomphe was built in 1836 to honor the great battles won by Napoleon Bonaparte, the army general who became Emperor of France in 1804. Parisians still gather at the 164-foot-high arch when there is a French victory to celebrate.

Top Facts

- Notre Dame cathedral is regarded as the exact center of Paris. Distances on road signs are worked out from this spot.

- Paris is the birthplace of the movies. The first film was shown there in 1895.

- Around one fifth of France's entire population live in Paris and its suburbs.

Paris's most famous tourist attraction is the 1,063-foot-high Eiffel Tower.

Notre Dame

Notre Dame cathedral stands on Ile de la Cité, the larger of the two islands in the middle of the River Seine. The cathedral, whose name means "Our Lady," took almost 200 years to build and was completed in 1345.

Venice

Venice has canals instead of roads and boats instead of cars. People travel on waterbuses, catch water taxis, or hire rowing boats called gondolas. Even ambulances and fire engines have to use the waterways!

City of islands

Venice was founded 1,500 years ago when people settled on a group of small islands, driving wooden posts into the mudbanks and building their houses on top of these. This magical city is made up of 118 islands and is famous for its art treasures and magnificent buildings.

The Grand Canal

The Grand Canal is Venice's Main Street. It is 2 miles long and winds through the center of the city. Some of the buildings that line the canal date back to the 1100s. The Rialto Bridge is the oldest and most famous of the three bridges spanning the Grand Canal.

Europe

Venice

ITALY

Mediterranean Sea

Gondoliers

Those who want a relaxed canal journey travel by gondola, a rowing boat steered with a single oar by a gondolier.

Magical carnival

The Venice Carnival, with its elaborate costumes, is the highlight of the city's year. St. Mark's Square and the theaters burst into life with musical, theatrical, and acrobatic performances. The carnival is 800 years old, one of the most celebrated and fascinating events in Europe.

Did You Know?
Venice has over 400 bridges, more than any other city in the world.

Rome

Rome is called the "Eternal City" because of its long and rich history. It was the heart of one of the world's greatest empires, and later became the center of the Christian Church.

Vatican City

The city of Rome contains the Vatican City. This is the world's smallest state, with a population of around a thousand people. It is led by the Pope, who is head of the Roman Catholic Church. Within Vatican City is St. Peter's Church, one of the holiest places for Roman Catholics. The church is huge; it has enough room for more than 60,000 people.

Top Facts

- The Romans gave us our calendar. Julius Caesar introduced the 365-day year.
- Rome is named after Romulus, son of the god Mars.

St. Peter's Church

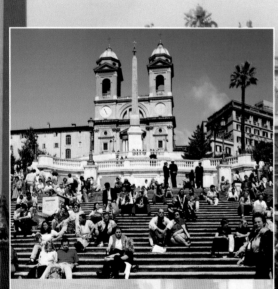

Spanish Steps

The Spanish Steps is an elegant, sweeping stairway leading up to the church of Trinita dei Monti. It gets its name from the Spanish Embassy, which is nearby.

The Colosseum

The Colosseum provided entertainment for the bloodthirsty Ancient Romans. It could hold 50,000 people, who watched gladiators, slaves, and criminals fight to the death. Five thousand wild animals were killed when the first games were held there in A.D. 80. The arena was sometimes flooded so that mock sea battles could be fought.

Europe

ITALY

• Rome

Mediterranean Sea

Did You Know?

Vatican City has its own radio station, hospital, and fire department—even its own money with the Pope's head on it.

The Trevi Fountain

The Trevi Fountain has a statue of Neptune, god of the sea, in a chariot pulled by two seahorses. One of the seahorses is wild, the other is calm, showing the different moods of the sea.

Jerusalem

Jerusalem is a holy city to three world religions. Jews believe that the city and surrounding land were promised to them by God. Christians believe Jesus Christ was crucified and buried there. Muslims believe it is the place where the Prophet Mohammed ascended to Heaven.

Capital city

For centuries Jews were moved from the land around Jerusalem to all parts of the world. They wanted to return to their homeland, and this led to the creation of the country of Israel in 1948, with Jerusalem as its capital. This land had been owned by Muslim Arabs, and the foundation of Israel led to a conflict, which is still not settled.

Wailing Wall

The Western Wall is Judaism's holiest shrine. Also known as the Wailing Wall, it is all that remains of the temple built to house the Ten Commandments.

The Wailing Wall

Top Facts

- Jerusalem today is a city of 700,000 people. There are around 460,000 Jews, 225,000 Muslims, and 15,000 Christians.

- Jews often place notes into the cracks of the Wailing Wall. These are prayers that they hope will be answered.

The Mount of Olives

Christians believe Jesus ascended to Heaven from the Mount of Olives. Nearby is the Garden of Gethsemane, where Jesus prayed before being arrested by the Romans.

Dome of the Rock

The Dome of the Rock is the world's oldest Muslim monument, built in A.D. 691. It is from here that the Prophet Mohammed is said to have ridden to Heaven on a winged horse. A mosque, which can still be seen, was built to protect the rock.

Church of the Holy Sepulchre

The Church of the Holy Sepulchre is the most important site for Christians. They believe this is built on the place where Jesus was crucified and buried and rose from the dead. The original church, built in the 400s, was destroyed. The present church dates from the 1100s.

Mediterranean Sea

Jerusalem ●

Asia

ISRAEL

Istanbul

Istanbul is the only city to be built over two continents. It is split by a channel of water called the Bosphorus Strait, with Europe on one side and Asia on the other. Istanbul was the center of two great historic empires, the Roman Empire and the Byzantine Empire.

Naming the city

The city of Istanbul has had many different names. It became known as Constantinople after Emperor Constantine made it the capital of the Roman Empire. The city was renamed Istanbul after it became part of the Ottoman Empire in the 1400s.

The Blue Mosque with its six minarets

Hagia Sophia

Hagia Sophia was a place of worship. It was originally a Christian church built in the 700s. It was turned it into a mosque when Istanbul became part of the Muslim Ottoman Empire. Today it is a museum.

The Bazaar

The Grand Bazaar is the world's oldest shopping mall, dating back over 500 years. This huge building contains 5,000 shops spread out along 60 streets. The shop owners need to sell a lot of goods to pay rents of up to 15 pounds of gold per year.

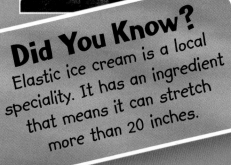

Did You Know?

Elastic ice cream is a local speciality. It has an ingredient that means it can stretch more than 20 inches.

The Blue Mosque

The Blue Mosque gets its name from the 20,000 colored tiles that cover the internal walls. Its six minarets caused a stir when it was built because only the Great Mosque in Mecca was supposed to have so many.

Beijing

In the last 50 years Beijing has changed from a medieval walled city into a modern industrial capital. Fifteen million people live in a city where ancient wooden palaces stand alongside modern buildings.

The Forbidden City

For 500 years China's emperors ruled the country from Beijing's Forbidden City, a vast walled area that ordinary people weren't allowed to enter. The last emperor, Puyi, was three years old when he came to power in 1908. The Chinese people decided they wanted a new system of government and Puyi left the imperial palace in 1912.

The Forbidden City

The National Stadium

The 2008 Olympics

China did not enter the Olympic Games until 1980, but there were great celebrations when Beijing was named the host city for 2008. The National Stadium, which was built especially for the Olympic Games, became known as the "bird's nest" among local people because of its shape.

Did You Know?
It takes a team of decorators 10 years to repair and paint the Forbidden City's 8,000 rooms.

Tiananmen Square

Tiananmen Square is the world's largest public square. It measures 875 yards by 545 yards and so it isn't really a square! A million people turn out there for great celebratory occasions, such as China's National Day on October 1.

Top Fact

- 8 August 2008 (08/08/08) was chosen as the starting date for the Olympic Games because the Chinese regard 8 as the luckiest number.

The Beijing Opera

Beijing Opera is based on Chinese legends. The plays include acrobatics and mime, as well as singing and dancing. There are four main role types: male and female parts, clowns, and characters with painted faces. The color of the face paint indicates the character. For example, a face painted red (shown above) represents bravery and loyalty.

Hong Kong

Hong Kong is an island city where Eastern and Western cultures meet. It is now part of China but was a British colony for 150 years. It is both a modern industrial city and a place where ancient Chinese customs are followed.

Feng shui

The city's skyscrapers are built using the ancient art of feng shui. This involves positioning buildings so that they receive positive energy and keep bad spirits away. Many buildings have been constructed on land reclaimed from the sea so Hong Kong's coastline has changed dramatically. For example, a temple that was once on the coast is now 1.8 miles inland!

Top Facts

- Hong Kong includes 236 islands as well as a mainland area. The city's name means "fragrant harbor."

- The world's steepest railroad runs to the top of Victoria Peak, the city's highest point. Cables powered by electric motors have pulled the tram up the 600-yard hill since 1880.

CHINA

Pacific Ocean

Asia

Hong Kong

Indian Ocean

Chinese junks

Flat-bottomed boats called junks, like the one above, have been sailing the coast of China for centuries. Luxury junks up to 75 feet long are used for parties and pleasure cruises.

Wealthiest Chinese city

Hong Kong is a global center for trade and is the wealthiest area in China. Hong Kong's population grew quickly in the 1990s and is just over 7 million today. The city is crowded, and most people live in high-rise apartments.

Tian Tan Buddha

Po Lin Monastery has the world's largest outdoor bronze statue of the seated Buddha. The Tian Tan Buddha is over 98 feet high and weighs over 200 tons. A bell inside the statue rings 108 times per day, representing escape from the "108 troubles of mankind" that Buddha identified.

Did You Know?

The scaffolding used in the building of the city's skyscrapers is made of bamboo sticks tied together with strips of plastic.

Sydney

Sydney today is a beautiful, modern city, but 200 years ago people who committed crimes in England were sent there as a punishment. The first convict ships arrived in 1788, and the British flag was raised in Sydney Harbor. Native Aborigines had lived in Australia for thousands of years, and now had to share their homeland.

Bondi Beach

Australians and tourists flock to Bondi Beach for the sun and surf. Surfing arrived in the city in 1914, when a visitor from Hawaii amazed local people with his ability to ride the waves on a board. Since then surfing has become a very popular sport throughout Australia.

Sydney Harbor

Sydney grew to become the largest city in Australia, though Canberra was chosen as the capital. The famous harbor splits Sydney in two. The two sides were joined in 1932 when the Sydney Harbour Bridge was opened. The many beaches are popular almost all year round as Sydney enjoys a warm, sunny climate.

The architect said that the roof design of the Sydney Opera House was inspired by peeling an orange.

Top Facts

- The world's first life-savers began work on Bondi Beach in 1906.

- Australians call Sydney Harbor Bridge "The Coathanger" because of its shape. Today there is a tunnel under the harbor, so the bridge is not so important for transport.

The Opera House

Sydney Opera House is one of the world's most famous buildings. There are five separate theaters inside the building, where people can see operas, plays, and ballets and hear concerts. The largest building is the concert hall (above).

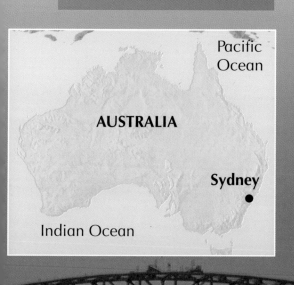

Pacific Ocean

AUSTRALIA

Sydney

Indian Ocean

Did You Know?

An English explorer called Matthew Flinders suggested naming the country Australia, from the Latin word meaning "southern." Before then it was called New Holland.

Las Vegas

Las Vegas is the entertainment capital of the world. Its main street, called "The Strip," is packed with hotels that are more like theme parks. One has a Parisian theme, complete with its own Eiffel Tower. Another has a volcano that erupts every 15 minutes!

Gambling center

Las Vegas is America's youngest major city. It was founded 100 years ago, when the railroad was built there. It grew quickly after 1931, when gambling was made legal. Most of the hotels have casinos where people play games such as roulette, bet on card games, and use slot machines. The casinos put on spectacular shows to keep their guests at the gambling tables.

Top Facts

- Las Vegas is the only city in the world with over 100,000 hotel rooms.

- Casinos don't have clocks. The owners want people to carry on gambling, not worry if it's past their bedtime.

- Las Vegas means "the meadows" in Spanish.

- Stratosphere Tower has the world's highest thrill ride, over 980 feet in the air.

State of Nevada

Las Vegas

UNITED STATES OF AMERICA

Pacific Ocean

Atlantic Ocean

Getting married

Over 100,000 couples get married in Las Vegas every year, many in fancy dress. You can buy a license to get married at almost any hour of the day, and there is even a drive-in wedding service.

Did You Know?
If all the city's neon lights were laid in a row they would stretch over 14,900 miles, farther than from England to Australia.

Spectacular sights

Las Vegas offers many spectacular sights. One hotel has 1,000 fountains that dance in time to music, with the water shooting 80 yards into the air. Another has its own pyramid, with a powerful beam of light shining from the top that can be seen from outer space.

New York City

New York has one of the most recognizable skylines of any city. The world's first skyscraper was built there in 1902. The Statue of Liberty in New York harbor is a symbol of the freedom and opportunity that the USA values so highly.

Manhattan

New York was originally ruled by the Dutch and called New Amsterdam. In 1664 the British took over and it was renamed New York. Today five large districts make up New York City, but it is the island of Manhattan that attracts most tourists. Manhattan has many famous landmarks, museums, and shops. Wall Street in Manhattan is the financial center of the USA.

The Statue of Liberty

The Statue of Liberty was built in 1886. It was a gift from France to mark the 100th anniversary of American independence.

New York State

New York City

UNITED STATES
OF AMERICA

Pacific
Ocean

Atlantic
Ocean

Central Park

Twenty million people a year visit Central Park, a 1.3-square-mile park that contains a lake, a zoo, and a museum as well as many sporting facilities, such as an outdoor ice rink in winter.

Did You Know?

The city is famous for its yellow taxi cabs. There are 12,000 of them!

Times Square

Times Square is the center of New York's entertainment district. The Broadway theaters nearby are famous the world over, and the Square's electric billboards are themselves a popular tourist attraction.

Top Facts

- New York is home to Macy's, the world's largest department store. It was just a corner shop when it was founded in 1857.

- New York is called the "Big Apple." It was given its nickname by jazz musicians in the 1930s.

Rio de Janeiro

If you like parties, Rio de Janeiro in Brazil has the biggest of them all. It is called Carnival and takes place in February or March each year.

Carnival

The highlight of the Carnival is the colorful parade. Thousands of people, dressed in elaborate costumes which are often decorated with feathers, sequins, mirrors, or metal, dance to samba music. As soon as the party is over, many people start making costumes for the next Carnival.

Top Facts

- Rio de Janeiro means "River of January." The Portuguese explorers who named it arrived in January 1502.

- Rio de Janeiro was the capital of Brazil until 1960, when a new city, Brasilia, was given that honor.

- Carnival takes place just before Lent, when Christians often give up certain foods. The people want to have a good time first.

Did You Know?

On New Year's Eve people throw gifts into the sea. They hope the Sea Goddess will bring them luck for the next year.

Atlantic Ocean

South America

BRAZIL

Rio de Janeiro

Pacific Ocean

Rio's Beaches

Rio has a 30-mile coastline and many beautiful beaches. The most famous of these is Copacabana. Football, volleyball, and surfing are popular pastimes on this 2½-mile stretch of white sand.

Rio's famous statue

Rio's most famous landmark is the statue of Jesus Christ, which overlooks the city from the top of Corcovado mountain. The 130-foot-high statue, called Christ the Redeemer, was built in 1931. The local people like to think the statue's outstretched arms are embracing and protecting the city.

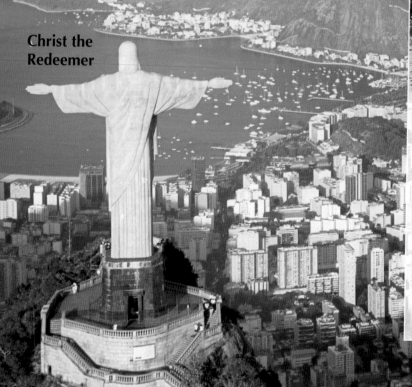

Christ the Redeemer

The Maracana

The Maracana is one of the largest and most famous stadiums in the world. Over 180,000 people once watched a football match there. Now it is an all-seater stadium holding 95,000. Pop concerts take place there as well as sporting events.

PEOPLE AND PLACES

Many explorers, artists, and rulers have become famous for one special achievement in a particular place. In this section, we look at amazing people and the spectacular landmarks their names will be forever linked with. One king spent over half of his 72-year reign building an extraordinary palace, while another built a castle so fabulous it was copied for a Disney film. Find out about the sculptor who carved a mountain, the prisoner who became president of his country, and the emperor who was buried with an army to protect him in the afterlife!

Hadrian's Wall

Hadrian's Wall was one of the best defended frontiers of the Roman Empire. It was so well built that much of it still stands today.

Building the wall

When Emperor Hadrian first visited Britain in A.D. 122 he ordered the construction of the wall. Hadrian wanted to defend Roman Britain against the strong warrior tribes of Scotland. Roman soldiers worked for 10 years to build the wall. It stretched for 74 miles from one side of Britain to the other. Soldiers lived in forts that were built all the way along the wall.

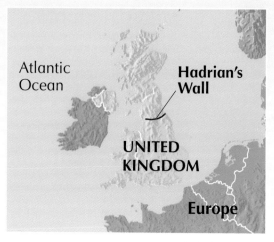

Atlantic Ocean

Hadrian's Wall

UNITED KINGDOM

Europe

Did You Know?
An Ancient Roman birthday invitation has been found at Hadrian's Wall.

Top Facts

- In some places the wall is so wide and strong that you can walk on top of it.
- Originally the wall would have been painted white so it would have looked even more impressive.

Hadrian

Hadrian was one of Rome's greatest emperors, but he did not like living in Rome. Instead he spent most of his time traveling across the Empire. Hadrian did not conquer new countries but he wanted the borders of the existing empire to be well defended.

Drain

Roman toilets

For many Roman soldiers, Britain was not a popular destination. It was remote and cold. To make life easier the soldiers built toilets, baths, temples, and other home comforts. At Housesteads Fort on Hadrian's Wall you can see the remains of Roman toilets. The seats were built above the drains, which you can see around the edge of the room. The Romans used sponges on sticks instead of toilet paper.

Anne Frank's house

When Anne Frank was given a diary for her 13th birthday she could have had no idea that this diary would be published—and that because of it she would become one of the most famous people in the 20th century.

Top Facts

- The house where Anne hid from the Nazis was turned into a museum in 1960.
- Of the eight people who were in the attic with Anne, only her father, Otto, survived the war.

Europe at war

Between 1938 and 1942, while Anne and her family were living in Amsterdam, Hitler's Nazi army invaded much of Europe. Many Jewish people, like Anne, were sent to prisons called concentration camps. Anne's family hid from the invading army with the help of their non-Jewish friends.

Anne's hiding place

In June 1942 Anne Frank's family, along with four other Jewish people, went into hiding in the attic of a house in Amsterdam. The entrance to the attic was covered by a large bookcase. Those in hiding were kept alive for two years by four friends who risked their lives to bring food to the attic. The secret place was eventually discovered and Anne and the others were sent to concentration camps.

Did You Know?
Anne's diary has been published in 55 languages and has sold more than 25 million copies worldwide.

Anne Frank

Anne Frank was born in 1929 in Germany, but left to escape Hitler's Nazi government when she was four years old. Her family moved to Amsterdam, but in 1942 Hitler's army arrived there. Anne spent seven months in a concentration camp after she was caught. She died from a disease called typhus in March 1945, just weeks before the prisoners were rescued.

The diary

Throughout her time in hiding, Anne wrote in her diary about her life, her feelings, and her dreams. Anne's descriptions give us a vivid picture of her life. She addressed her diary as if it were a person; she called it Kitty. The diary was saved and was published after the war.

Louis' palace at Versailles

Versailles was the biggest and most luxurious palace in the whole world when Louis XIV was finally satisfied with his new home. Building work started in 1669 and finished in 1710, taking 41 years to complete.

Top Facts

- The royal court moved to the palace in May 1682.

- There were so many fountains at Versailles that there was not enough water to have them all on at once. Only the fountains the king could see were turned on fully.

The palace and garden

The palace was like a small town. Thousands of people lived and worked there every day. The palace has around 700 rooms, which include apartments for the king and queen, rooms for the courtiers, and public rooms where the king would meet his court and important visitors. The palace is surrounded by 3 square miles of beautiful gardens. These were carefully designed so that everything was symmetrical.

The Hall of Mirrors

The most famous room in the palace is the Hall of Mirrors. Along one side of this long room are 17 huge windows that look out over the gardens. Along the opposite wall are 17 large mirrors. The room was designed to display the king's power and glory. Louis used this room to meet foreign leaders so he could show off his wealth and the grandeur of the French court.

King Louis XIV

Louis XIV was one of the most powerful kings in history. He reigned from 1643 until 1715—a total of 72 years. He was just four years old when he became king, so a powerful nobleman ruled in his place until he became an adult. Louis XIV was known as the "Sun King." One of the reasons that he chose this title was because the Sun was the symbol of Apollo, who was one of the most powerful and important Greek gods.

Did You Know?

The treaty that ended the First World War was signed in the Hall of Mirrors in 1919.

King Ludwig's fairytale castle

King Ludwig II of Bavaria built his beautiful castle in the mountains, far from the royal court in Munich.

King Ludwig

Ludwig dreamed about being the heroic "swan knight" of an ancient German legend. He was inspired to build Neuschwanstein by a castle in that legend. Ludwig began to spend all his time at his castle instead of ruling Bavaria and in 1886 the government decided to declare Ludwig insane. Just one day later he was found dead in mysterious circumstances. He was only 40 when he died.

Top Facts

- Building began in 1869 and took many years. The castle was still not finished when King Ludwig died 17 years later.

- Fourteen craftsmen spent four years carving the oak walls and furniture in the king's bedroom.

The model for Disney

The castle is one of the best-known places in the whole of Germany. It has also become famous around the world because Walt Disney used it as the model for the castle in his film *Cinderella*. Ludwig did not like strangers to visit his castle, so he probably would not have liked the fact that millions of tourists have visited since his death.

Inside the castle

The inside of the castle was decorated according to Ludwig's dreams. The walls were covered with images from German fairytales and legends. Many of these were told in the operas of the great composer Richard Wagner, who was a friend of the king and was an important influence on him. The castle might look very old, but Ludwig made sure it had all the latest inventions of the day. These included telephones, lifts, flushing toilets, central heating, and electricity.

Gaudí's Barcelona

The city of Barcelona in Spain is full of beautiful buildings, but those designed by Antoni Gaudi are known for their strange shapes and bright colors.

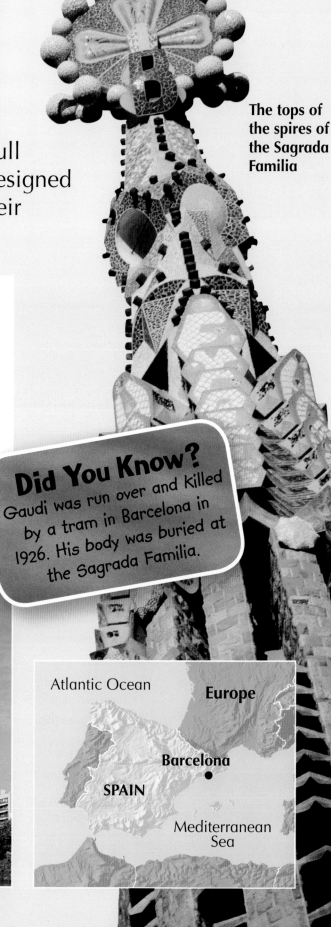

The tops of the spires of the Sagrada Familia

Gaudí's cathedral

Gaudi's greatest project was the Church of the Sagrada Familia, or Holy Family, in Barcelona. Work began in 1884 and it is still not finished. Gaudi was very religious and he wanted to build the church as a center for Catholic worship. In the later years of his life he stopped work on all his other projects and devoted himself to building the cathedral.

Did You Know?
Gaudi was run over and killed by a tram in Barcelona in 1926. His body was buried at the Sagrada Familia.

Atlantic Ocean

Europe

Barcelona

SPAIN

Mediterranean Sea

The Casa Batllo

Gaudi changed an ordinary looking house into something strange and wonderful. His idea was to create a building to tell the story of Saint George and the Dragon. The balconies look like the bones of the dragon's victims and the roof tiles are designed to look like a dragon's scales. Towering above the dragon is a cross, which represents Saint George.

In Guell Park the buildings and benches are oddly shaped and covered in mosaics.

Top Facts

- **The Sagrada Familia is still not completed. It is hoped it will be finished within 20 years.**
- **Guell Park is named after Eusebi Guell. He provided the money for several of Gaudi's works.**

Tutankhamun's tomb

After searching in the Valley of the Kings for seven years, the archaeologist Howard Carter discovered 16 steps that led to a sealed door. Inside he found the tomb of the Ancient Egyptian pharaoh Tutankhamun.

Discovering the tomb

Howard Carter discovered the sealed doorway on November 4, 1922. However, he had to wait 20 days for the arrival of Lord Carnarvon, a wealthy Englishman who had paid him to search for the tomb, before the seals on the door could be broken. When Carter eventually shone a candle into the tomb and saw that it was full of objects, he realized that he had found something special. When Lord Carnarvon asked if he could see anything, the amazed Carter could only reply, "Yes, wonderful things."

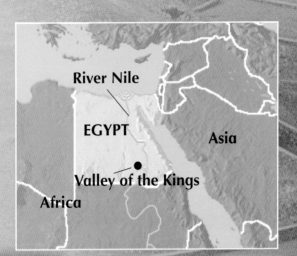

River Nile

EGYPT

Asia

Valley of the Kings

Africa

Did You Know?
Tutankhamun's tomb was thought to be cursed. Two people involved in opening up the tomb died suddenly. However, most people who took part in the dig went on to live long lives.

Jewelry
Howard Carter found nearly 150 pieces of jewelry in the cloth that was wrapped around Tutankhamun's body.

The treasures

Almost all of the tombs in the Valley of the Kings had been robbed before archaeologists arrived. However, most of Tutankhamun's treasures were still there. Jewels, thrones, weapons, furniture, and statues were found. Most incredible of all were Tutankhamun's three coffins and the magnificent gold mask, decorated with a blue stone called lapis lazuli, that covered the pharaoh's head.

Howard Carter

Howard Carter was born in London in 1874. It was his love of drawing that took him to Egypt in 1891, where his first job was to copy the artwork found in the ancient tombs. He soon became involved in archaeology and began digging in the Valley of the Kings in 1915. Here he is shown with an assistant cleaning Tutankhamun's coffins.

Nelson Mandela's island prison

Robben Island in South Africa is one of the most famous prisons in the world. For many years people who did not agree with the ideas of the South African government were imprisoned there. Probably the most famous prisoner was Nelson Mandela.

The island

Robben Island is less than 9 miles away from the busy city of Cape Town. From 1836 to 1931 people with leprosy were sent to the island to keep them away from the city. It was also a good place to put a prison because it was surrounded by stormy seas and shark-infested waters. This meant that very few people ever managed to escape.

Top Facts
- Robben Island means "Seal Island." When the Europeans first arrived the island was home to many seals.
- Nelson Mandela was known as prisoner 46664 during his 27 years in prison.
- Robben Island is only around 1100 yards wide and is just a few yards above sea level.

Africa

Cape Town SOUTH AFRICA Indian Ocean

• Robben Island

Nelson Mandela

Nelson Mandela was one of the leaders in the fight against the South African government's policy of "apartheid," the idea that people with different skin colors should not be allowed to live side by side. In 1964 Mandela was sent to prison on the island for protesting against this idea. He was kept in jail for 27 years. He was released in 1990 and was elected President of South Africa in 1994.

Did You Know?

The prison was closed in the 1990s. Today the island is a museum where you can learn about apartheid. Many of the museum guides were once prisoners on the island.

The prison

Nelson Mandela's cell measured 54 square feet, and he was allowed only one visitor and one letter every six months. During the day he worked in a quarry, where the glare from the white limestone damaged his eyes. When Mandela became president, he forgave the guards who ill-treated him and invited them to a state banquet.

Hillary and Tenzing conquer Everest

At 29,000 feet, Mount Everest is the highest mountain on Earth. Many people have lost their lives trying to climb it.

The Himalayas

The Himalayas is the greatest mountain range in the world. Most of the tallest 100 mountains in the world are found there. The Himalayas stretches 1,550 miles from China in the east to Afghanistan in the west. It is made up of lots of smaller mountain ranges, including the Karakorams, which is home to the world's second-highest mountain, K2.

Top Facts

- George Mallory and Andrew Irvine were the first Western people to try to climb Everest. Sadly, they both died on the mountain.

- Mount Everest is the tallest mountain above sea level. However, it is not the tallest from the ocean floor. That honor goes to Mauna Kea in Hawaii.

Afghanistan   NEPAL   China

India

Mount Everest

Indian Ocean

Mount Everest

Edmund Hillary

Edmund Hillary was born in New Zealand in 1919. He worked as a beekeeper, but spent all his spare time climbing mountains near his home. He wanted to be first to conquer the highest mountain in the world. Through his daring and determination he succeeded and reached the top of Everest on May 29, 1953.

Mount Everest

Mount Everest was named by Sir Andrew Waugh when he was sent by the British to draw maps of India. He named the mountain after Sir George Everest, who had also worked for the British government. The mountain has several local names. The sherpas call it "Chomolungma," which means "goddess of the snows." "Sagarmatha," meaning "on top of the world," is the name given to it by the government of Nepal in the 1960s.

Did You Know?

In 2004 a sherpa called Pemba Darji climbed to the top of Everest in just over eight hours.

Sherpa Tenzing Norgay

Tenzing Norgay was Edmund Hillary's guide on the climb in 1953. He was a sherpa, which is the name given to people who live near Mount Everest. Sherpas have guided people around the Himalayas for many years. Today, many more people attempt to climb the mountain each year. It is still very dangerous and climbers often lose their lives.

The Dalai Lama's hilltop palace

The great Potala Palace of the Dalai Lama sits on a hill above the city of Lhasa in Tibet. It is an important center for the Buddhist religion.

The palace

A palace was first built here in the 600s by the Tibetan king Songsten Gampo. He is thought to be one of Tibet's greatest rulers because he made his country powerful and brought Buddhism to its people. The original palace was destroyed by fire and war. The palace we can see today was built more than 400 years ago.

Top Facts

- Eight Dalai Lamas are buried in the grounds of the palace. Many of their tombs are covered in jewels and vast amounts of gold.

- The palace is open to the public as a museum.

The Dalai Lama

The Dalai Lama is the ruler and religious leader of Tibet. There have been 14 since the first one was born in 1391. Buddhists believe that each Dalai Lama is the reincarnation of the previous one. When the Dalai Lama dies, Buddhists begin the search for his reborn spirit. It is usually discovered in a young boy, who is taken to the palace to train to continue the work of the previous ruler.

The current Dalai Lama lives in India because China now rules Tibet. He hopes that one day he will be able to return to the Potala Palace.

Did You Know?
The death of the fifth Dalai Lama was kept secret for 15 years so that the Potala Palace could be finished before the new Dalai Lama was appointed.

Inside the palace

The Potala Palace is divided into two sections, the Red Palace and the White Palace. They are named after the colors of the walls. The Red Palace is the religious center. In it there are more than 10,000 places to worship and it is a place where Buddhist monks are trained. The White Palace is where the Dalai Lamas lived and from where they ruled Tibet.

The Terracotta Warriors

In 1974 some farmers digging a well near Xi'an in central China made an incredible discovery. Buried beneath the ground were hundreds of life-size model soldiers that were more than 2,000 years old.

Qin Shi Huangdi

The soldiers were made to protect the tomb of the Emperor Qin Shi Huangdi, who ruled from 221 until 210 B.C. Qin Shi Huangdi is one of the most important rulers in Chinese history. Before he came to power, China was divided into small warring states. He brought them together and became the first Emperor of all China.

Top Facts

- The emperor is buried close to where the soldiers were found. However, archaeologists have not yet looked inside his tomb.

- We know the names of some of the craftsmen who built the warriors because they wrote them on their work.

CHINA

Xi'an

Pacific Ocean

Asia

Indian Ocean

The soldiers

Amazingly each of the Chinese warriors is different. Some are taller or fatter than others and they have different hairstyles, facial expressions, and costumes. The warriors were made from a type of clay called terracotta. Originally they were painted in bright colors, but the paint has worn away over time.

An army of soldiers

Together the soldiers formed an army to protect the emperor in the afterlife. There are at least 7,000 figures, but there may be many more. The model soldiers are dressed in different uniforms to show what part they played in the army.

Pottery jigsaw

Most of the soldiers had broken into pieces over the years. Archaeologists have had to put them back together like a jigsaw. Many have been restored so we can see what they would have looked like 2,000 years ago. However, there are many soldiers that are still broken.

159

Gutzon Borglum's Mount Rushmore

Mount Rushmore in the Black Hills of South Dakota is a monument to freedom and democracy. Carved into the hillside are sculptures of four American presidents.

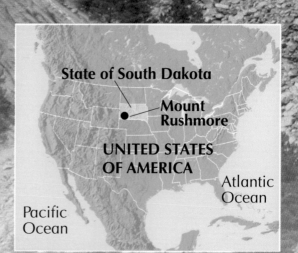

Did You Know?

Gutzon Borglum began by making a model that was 12 times smaller than the planned sculpture. This was used as a guide for the workmen.

The monument

The monument was designed by a sculptor named Gutzon Borglum. Borglum needed more than 400 men to help him build it. First the workmen used dynamite to blast the rock into the right shape. Then they were lowered down from the top of the mountain on strong steel cables so that they could carve the face of each president. Work began in 1927 and took around 15 years to complete.

State of South Dakota

Mount Rushmore

UNITED STATES OF AMERICA

Pacific Ocean

Atlantic Ocean

The presidents

The four presidents are (left to right) George Washington, Thomas Jefferson, Theodore Roosevelt, and Abraham Lincoln. These presidents are often considered to be the greatest in American history. Together they helped shape the first 150 years of the nation from the Declaration of Independence to the 20th century.

Gutzon Borglum

Gutzon Borglum was born in the American state of Idaho in 1867. He studied sculpture in Paris but returned to the United States, where he created many important monuments. Borglum was 60 years old when he started work on Mount Rushmore. It took up the rest of his life. He died in 1941, leaving his son, Lincoln, to finish the job.

Borglum's plan

Theodore Roosevelt's was the last head to be completed, in 1939. Borglum's plan was to carve the body of each president as well as their heads, but there was not enough money to do this.

Hiram Bingham and Machu Picchu

In 1911 Hiram Bingham discovered the remains of an Inca city. It was hidden high in the Andes Mountains and had been forgotten about for years.

The Inca people

During the 1400s, the Inca people ruled over one of the largest empires in South American history. It stretched across the west of the continent and was joined together by a network of roads. The Incas were good builders and farmers and they were also very religious.

Top Facts

- Machu Picchu has more than 100 stairways carved from solid stone.

- After discovering Machu Picchu, Hiram Bingham went on to join the army during the First World War. He then became a politician in America.

Sacred Plaza

Central Plaza

Condor Temple

Royal Tomb

Funeral Rock Hut

Inca Trail

The settlement is 8,200 feet above sea level but the Incas managed to transport enough materials to build temples, palaces, baths, and tombs as well as houses there.

Machu Picchu

When the Spanish arrived in Inca territory early in the 1500s they completely destroyed most Inca cities. But they never discovered Machu Picchu and many of the buildings have survived to show us how the Incas lived. Machu Picchu was probably a summer palace used by the Inca kings to get away from the busy cities of their empire.

Did You Know?

The Inca people did not use wheels for transport and it is thought that all the stone for the city was carried up to the mountaintop.

Hiram Bingham

Hiram Bingham was a teacher at an American university but loved exploring. He made it his goal to find Vilcabamba, the "lost capital city of the Incas." During his exploration, Bingham discovered Machu Picchu and thought he had found what he was looking for. Machu Picchu was not the "lost capital," but it is the most impressive Inca settlement ever discovered.

ASTONISHING STRUCTURES

Strong feelings and deep beliefs have been the inspiration behind some of the world's most spectacular buildings. In this section, we look at how religion, friendship, grief, and fear have led to some amazing structures being built. Find out about the mosque that is made from mud and the people so afraid of invaders that they built a 3,700-mile wall to keep them out. Learn about the emperor who was so upset when his wife died that he ordered 2,000 people to spend 20 years building her a magnificent tomb!

The Eiffel Tower

When it was built in 1889, the Eiffel Tower was the tallest structure in the world. The tower weighs around 7,200 tons and is made from over 18,000 pieces of iron.

Why was the tower built?

The Eiffel Tower was built for the 1889 Universal Exposition in Paris. The Exposition, or exhibition, was arranged to celebrate the 100th anniversary of the French Revolution. The French government wanted the rest of the world to marvel at their great work made from iron, but many Parisians were afraid that it would collapse on the city. Alexandre Gustave Eiffel, the engineer who was building the tower, continued his work, confident that it would be safe.

Building the tower
It took 250 men just over two years to build the Eiffel Tower.

Top Facts

- The Eiffel Tower is 1,000 feet high. It was the tallest structure in the world until 1930.
- The whole tower is repainted every seven years.

Alexandre Gustave Eiffel

Eiffel was one of France's greatest engineers, and built many bridges. Eiffel's experience of working with metal bridges helped him calculate how the tower should be constructed so that it did not collapse or blow about in the wind. Eiffel also used his understanding of metals to design the framework for the Statue of Liberty.

Visiting the tower

There are 1,665 steps to the top of the tower. Today you can only climb as high as the third floor and then you have to take a lift the rest of the way up. The tower welcomes six million tourists each year. More than 200 million people have visited it since it was built.

Red Square

Red Square in the center of Moscow is home to some of the most spectacular and important buildings in Russia.

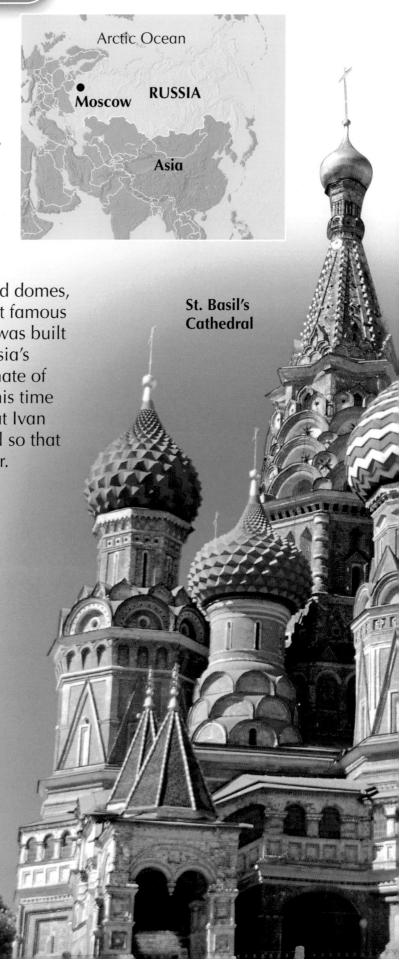

Arctic Ocean

Moscow **RUSSIA**

Asia

St. Basil's Cathedral

St. Basil's Cathedral

With its brightly colored onion-shaped domes, St. Basil's Cathedral is one of the most famous monuments in Russia. The cathedral was built in the 1550s and commemorates Russia's victory over its great enemy, the Khanate of Kazan. The Russian tsar, or ruler, at this time was Ivan the Terrible and it is said that Ivan blinded the architects of the cathedral so that they could never build anything better.

The domes

St. Basil's Cathedral is decorated with eight colorful domes.

The Kremlin

The city of Moscow was originally built within a medieval fortress called the Kremlin. It was protected from invaders by a great wall, more than 6,500 feet long. Inside the walls are palaces, cathedrals, churches, and government buildings.

State Historical Museum

On the north side of Red Square is the State Historical Museum. It was built at the end of the 1800s and opened in 1894. The museum contains many millions of objects from Russia's past.

The Leaning Tower of Pisa

The world-famous tower of Pisa's cathedral began to lean almost as soon as it was built. At almost 197 feet tall and weighing nearly 15,000 tons, perhaps that is not surprising.

The bell tower

Building began on the cathedral's bell tower in 1173. Work was slow because the city of Pisa was so often at war, and it took almost 200 years to complete the tower. The tower began to lean, even before it was complete, because its foundations were too shallow and the earth it is built on is too soft to support its weight.

In recent years, thousands of people have climbed to the top of the tower and made the tilt greater. Engineers have used modern technology to reduce the lean slightly but the tower cannot be straightened.

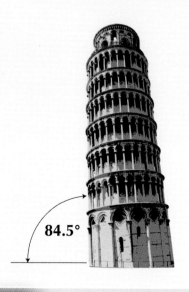

84.5°

The angle

If the tower stood straight, the angle between the tower and the ground would be 90 degrees on each side. Because it leans at an angle of 5.5 degrees, the angle between the tower and the ground is 95.5 degrees on one side and 84.5 degrees on the other.

Galileo Galilei's experiment

Legend says that the scientist Galileo Galilei performed one of his most famous experiments at Pisa. He is said to have dropped two objects of different weights from the top of the tower. Both objects hit the ground at almost the same time. This proved to him that the force of gravity causes everything to fall at the same rate—regardless of its weight.

The bells

To reach the top of the tower where there are seven large bells, you would have to climb 294 stairs—but the bells can be rung from the bottom of the tower using a bell rope.

Pisa Cathedral

Europe

● **Pisa**

ITALY

Mediterranean Sea

Did You Know?
Engineers have been trying to reduce the tower's lean since the Middle Ages.

171

The Alhambra

The Alhambra sits on a hill above the city of Granada in southern Spain. The fortress was the medieval palace of the Muslim rulers of Spain.

The palace

In the 1200s a Muslim king called Ibn al-Ahmar designed a magnificent new palace on the site of an existing fortress, where he and his family could live. He included huge towers and walls for protection. His son finished building the palace and their descendants decorated it lavishly. In the 1400s Christians conquered Granada, and when Emperor Carlos V became king in the 1500s he demolished part of the Alhambra and built his own palace there.

Top Facts

- **Water from the River Darro, 5 miles away, was diverted to provide the palace with a constant water supply.**

- **Napoleon's forces occupied the Alhambra in 1812. Luckily, their attempt to blow up the whole complex when they left was a failure.**

The gardens

The Muslim kings wanted the Alhambra to be the closest thing to paradise on Earth. The natural landscape of snowy mountain peaks and forests was already beautiful but the kings added carefully designed gardens and courtyards. These are decorated with fountains, statues, pools, plants, and trees.

Court of the Lions

One of the many beautiful courtyards is the Court of the Lions, which contains a fountain supported by 12 stone lions.

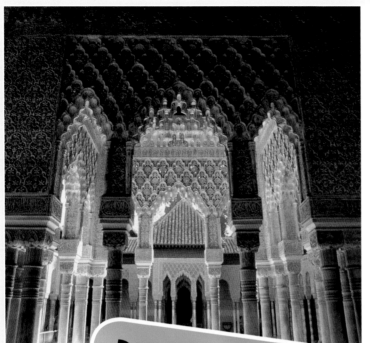

Decoration

From the outside the Alhambra looks like a strong fortress but on the inside it looks quite different. The rooms are decorated with complicated carvings, and slim columns hold up the ceilings. In some rooms the walls and floors are covered with colorful tiles, which are arranged to make repeating patterns.

Did You Know?
The word "Alhambra" comes from the Arabic word for "red." The palace was named after the color of the hill it sits on.

Atlantic Ocean

Europe

SPAIN

Granada

Mediterranean Sea

Africa

The Mud Mosque

The Great Mosque at Djenné in Mali is the largest mud brick building in the world. There has been a mosque in this place for centuries but work began on the present one in 1906.

Mud bricks

The Great Mosque was made from mudbricks that were baked in the sun until they became very hard. A plaster, also made of mud, was spread on top of the bricks to make the walls smooth. The walls are more than half a yard thick in places and are thickest where the building is tallest.

Top Facts

- The Great Mosque was built when the French ruled Djenné. They helped to fund some of the building work.

- There are wooden beams sticking out across the building. These are used as scaffolding when the local people repair the building.

Protecting the mosque

The local market is held in front of the mosque. The mosque is built on a platform above the level of the market so that it is protected from the flood waters of the nearby Bani River.

The festival

The people of Djenné join together to repair the building. Each year there is a great festival when everyone helps to plaster the walls of the mosque. Children bring water for the workers and help to mix the plaster. While the work goes on, the townspeople feast, dance, and play music.

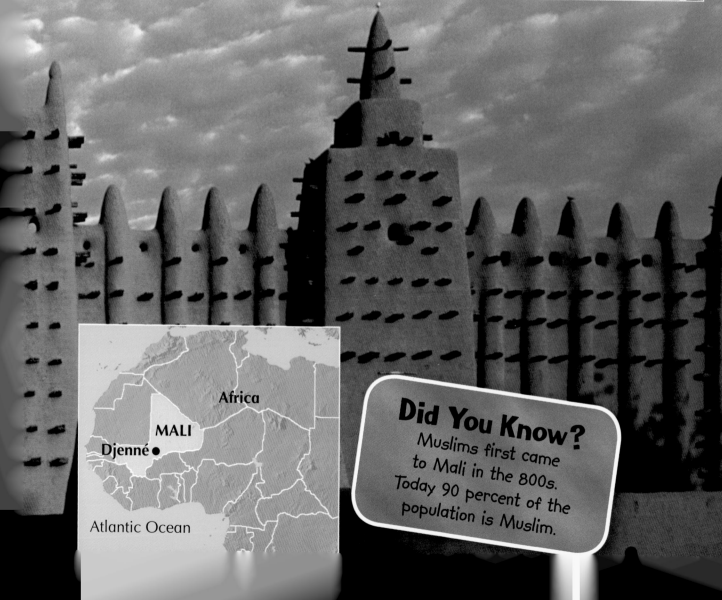

Africa

MALI

Djenné •

Atlantic Ocean

Did You Know?
Muslims first came to Mali in the 800s. Today 90 percent of the population is Muslim.

The Taj Mahal

The Taj Mahal in Agra, India, is a spectacular monument to eternal love. It was built by the Emperor Shah Jahan as a tomb for his favorite wife, Mumtaz.

Building the Taj Mahal

In 1632 Shah Jahan began work on the Taj Mahal. It took 20,000 people 22 years to complete the task. The tomb is reflected in a pool set in the beautiful gardens laid out in front of it. The gardens represent paradise and, like the building, they are perfectly symmetrical.

Top Facts

- The minarets at the corners of the building slope outward slightly. If an earthquake struck the area, the minarets would fall away from the tomb.

- The white marble that covers the Taj Mahal came from a quarry 185 miles away, carried on the backs of 1,000 elephants.

Did You Know?

The marble is cleaned following a recipe Indian women have used on their skin for centuries. The ingredients include milk and cereal.

Shah Jahan

Shah Jahan planned to build an identical tomb for himself in black marble facing the Taj Mahal. He was overthrown by his son, Aurangzeb, who kept him in prison for the last eight years of his life. To save money Aurangzeb ordered his father to be buried in a tomb beside Mumtaz in the Taj Mahal.

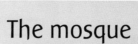

The mosque

There are several other small buildings in the gardens surrounding the Taj Mahal, including memorials to some of Shah Jahan's other wives. One of the most beautiful of these buildings is the mosque, which is made from red sandstone and decorated with marble.

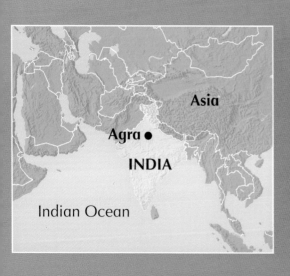

Asia

Agra ●

INDIA

Indian Ocean

The Golden Temple

The Golden Temple at Amritsar is the holiest shrine of the Sikh religion. Sikhism was founded around 500 years ago by Guru Nanak. He was the first of 10 Gurus, or teachers, who gave holy guidance to their followers.

The temple

The temple at Amritsar, called Harmandir Sahib (House of God) by the Sikhs, was built in 1601 by the fifth Guru, Arjan. This site was chosen because it is where Guru Nanak lived. Gold, marble, and precious jewels were used to decorate the temple. It was destroyed many times by invading armies, and had to be rebuilt.

The holy book

Inside the temple is Sikhism's holy book, called Guru Granth Sahib. When the 10th Guru died 300 years ago, he named this book as his successor instead of a person. Sikhs think of it as their living Guru.

Entering the temple

Visitors have to cross a bridge to reach the temple, which stands in the middle of a lake. Anyone may enter the building provided they remove their shoes and cover their head as a sign of respect.

Daily ritual

The holy book, Guru Granth Sahib, rests on a special platform called the Palki Sahib. It is covered by a golden canopy to show its importance. Every evening the sacred book is carried to a nearby building called Akal Takht. It is brought back to the temple each morning.

Top Fact

- Sikhs wear five items as a sign of their faith, all beginning with the letter K:
- *kesh* is the hair, which is never cut
- *kanga* is a comb to keep the hair tidy
- *kara* is a bracelet
- *kirpan* is a sword, which shows their readiness to fight for truth and justice
- *kaccha* are undershorts

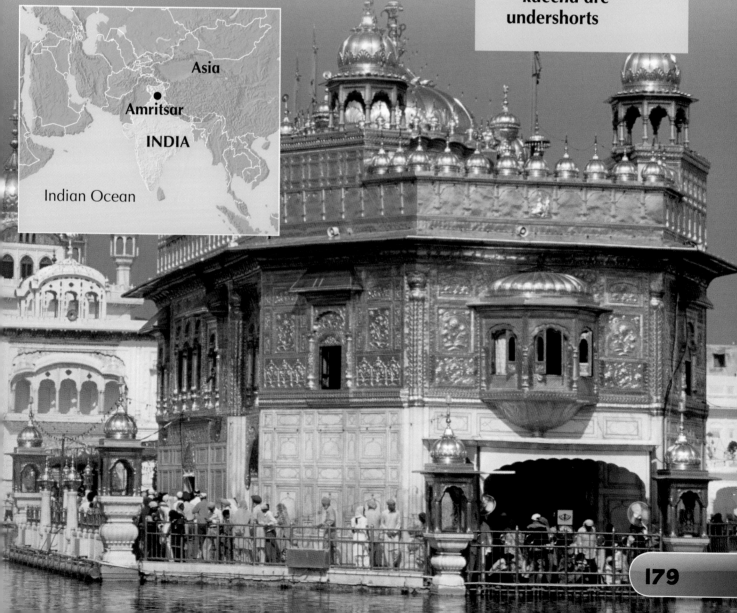

Asia

Amritsar

INDIA

Indian Ocean

The Great Wall of China

The Great Wall of China is the longest manmade object in the world. It winds for thousands of miles through China, crossing mountains, deserts, and marshland.

Building the wall

In the third century B.C. the Chinese Emperor Qin Shi Huang commanded the construction of a wall to protect his northern border. At this time many walls were already in place, but there were gaps between them that allowed invaders to get through. The emperor linked up these walls to make one Great Wall.

Watchtowers

Watchtowers were built all along the wall. Guards sent messages from one watchtower to the next using smoke signals.

Top Facts

- The Great Wall is 4,000 miles long and is 26 feet high in the best-preserved places.
- The Chinese conquered the territory to the north of the Great Wall 350 years ago, so it was no longer needed to defend their land.

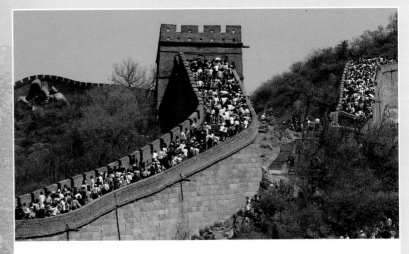

Great Wall

Asia   CHINA   Pacific Ocean

Indian Ocean

Marching armies

The wall was made wide enough for 10 soldiers to march side by side along the top. Five men on horseback could ride alongside one another. Today, there are many places where you can still see the wall and you can also walk along it.

The wall today

Some of the oldest sections of the wall have fallen into ruin and have almost disappeared. Other parts, which were built later with stronger materials, have been preserved and some have been reconstructed.

Angkor Wat

Angkor Wat is a huge ancient temple in Cambodia in southeast Asia. It was built almost 900 years ago but was later abandoned and lost for hundreds of years. It was rediscovered in the 1800s.

The temple

The temple of Angkor Wat was built in the 1100s by King Suryavarman II, the ruler of the Khmer Empire. Angkor Wat was originally a temple to the Hindu god Vishnu. The Khmer kings believed they were an earthly form of Vishnu and when Suryavarman died in 1150, he was buried inside the temple. After his death, Angkor Wat became a Buddhist place of worship.

A huge area

The temple buildings are surrounded by an outer wall that encloses an area of more than 860,000 square feet.

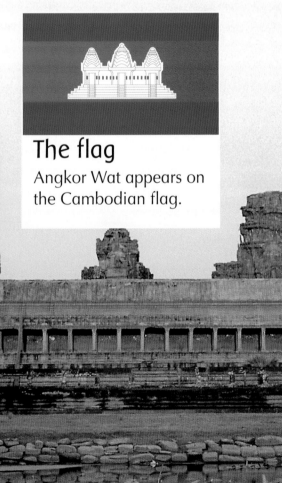

Rediscovery

After Angkor Wat was abandoned, the jungle crept in and hid the temple for 600 years. It was rediscovered in 1861 by a French explorer, Henri Mouhot.

The flag

Angkor Wat appears on the Cambodian flag.

- The temple is surrounded by a wide moat. Visitors have to cross a causeway to enter.

- The temple of Angkor Wat was part of an ancient city called Angkor. This was once the largest city in the ancient world.

Beautiful sculptures

Angkor Wat is famous for its sculptures. These are images cut into the stone walls that tell stories from Hindu mythology. The most popular are those of women dancing. These dancing girls are found all around the temple and are called *apsaras*.

Angkor Wat is surrounded by a moat.

Asia

● Angkor Wat

CAMBODIA

Indian Ocean

The Easter Island sculptures

The Easter Island heads are among the most mysterious stone statues in the world. We know very little about how they were made and about the people who made them.

The remote island

Easter Island lies in the Pacific Ocean. It is over 1,240 miles from the nearest inhabited island. People first settled on Easter Island around 1,000 years ago. On Easter Day 1722, the island was visited by a European ship and was given the name Easter Island. The people who live there call it Rapa Nui.

Did You Know?

The heads and ears of the sculptures are unusually long. Some of the ear lobes are pierced.

Top Facts

- There are over 800 statues on the island. About 230 of these are on platforms along the coast. Many others are unfinished and remain in the quarry.
- The huge sculptures were carved out of rock using stone tools.

The statues

The statues are called *moai* by the local people. They sit on stone platforms and some of them face out to sea. Most of the heads are between 13 and 16 feet high but there are some that are nearly twice as tall. Many heads have eyes made from white coral and black stone, and some have hats made from red stone. We do not know why the sculptures were made but they might represent dead ancestors.

How were the statues put in place?

No one is sure how the statues were moved from the place where they were quarried. Local legends say that the statues walked to their platforms. Experts have done experiments to test different ways of moving the stones. Dragging the heads with ropes and using wooden rollers to slide the statues into position were both successful methods. A new idea is that canoes were used as sledges.

Pacific Ocean

South America

EASTER ISLAND

Atlantic Ocean

The tallest stones are around 33 feet high —that's five times the height of a man.

The Statue of Liberty

One of the most famous landmarks in the United States of America is the Statue of Liberty. It has stood on Liberty Island at the entrance to New York Harbor since 1886.

A gift from France

The statue was a gift from France to America to celebrate 100 years of American independence. The sculptor Frédéric-Auguste Bartholdi created the statue. Inside the statue is an iron frame designed by Gustave Eiffel. There is a small version of the statue in Paris, which is around 30 feet tall.

Top Facts

- The whole structure is 305 feet high from the base of the pedestal to the tip of the torch.
- The Statue of Liberty was used as a lighthouse from 1886 until 1902. The light could be seen for nearly 25 miles.

Did You Know?

The statue was originally built in France and then taken apart, carried on a ship to New York, and reassembled there.

New York State

New York City

UNITED STATES OF AMERICA

Pacific Ocean

Atlantic Ocean

Ellis Island

For many years, immigrants arriving in the USA have thought of the Statue of Liberty as a welcome to a new life. Immigrants landed on Ellis Island, near Liberty Island. Here they were given health checks and their details were recorded before they were allowed to go to the mainland. Thousands of people landed here every day until the reception center on the island closed in 1954.

The Declaration of Independence

Liberty carries a tablet in her left hand on which the date July 4, 1776 is written. It was on this date that the United States of America was born, when leaders of 13 American colonies signed the Declaration of Independence. They declared they were independent states, free from rule by Great Britain.

Lady Liberty

The seven rays of Liberty's crown represent freedom spreading out across the world. There are broken chains at her feet, which symbolize freedom from cruel rulers. In one hand she holds a copy of the Declaration of Independence. The torch, which shines in the sunlight, guides people to the "land of the free."

Chichen Itza

Chichen Itza is a large city built by the Mayan people in the State of Yucatan in Mexico. The city was founded in around A.D. 850 and it developed during the next two or three centuries.

The pyramid

The Pyramid of Kukulcan, sometimes called El Castillo (the castle), is a stepped pyramid in the centre of Chichen Itza. It is over 80 feet high and has nine terraces and four staircases. The four-sided pyramid has steep stone steps on all sides. Each side is perfectly in line with the points of the compass: north, south, east, and west.

Top Facts

- There are 91 steep steps on each side of El Castillo pyramid.
- Chichen Itza has an observatory where the movements of the Sun, Moon, and stars were studied.

Did You Know?

Chichen Itza has a well, or cenote, where offerings were made to the rain god. Precious metals, sacred images, and the bones of human sacrifices have been found in the well.

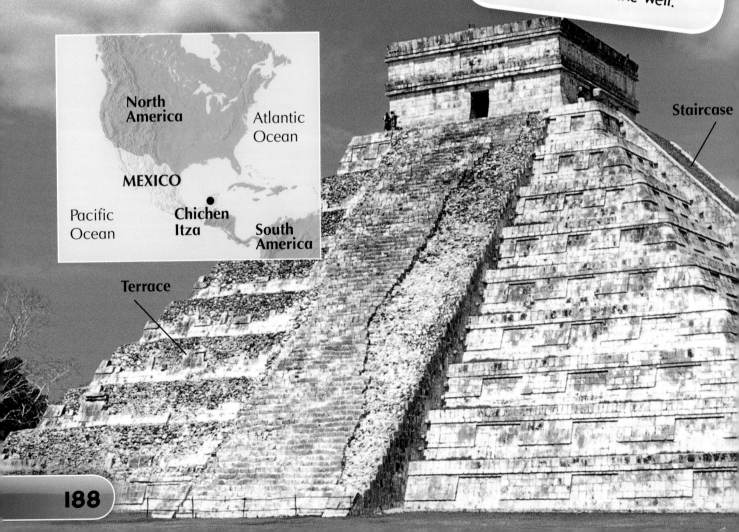

North America

Atlantic Ocean

MEXICO

Pacific Ocean

Chichen Itza

South America

Staircase

Terrace

Temple of the Warriors

We do not know what names the Mayans gave to their buildings at Chichen Itza. The names we use today were given by the Spanish settlers who arrived after the town had been abandoned by the Mayans. The Temple of the Warriors is named after the carvings of warriors on the pillars that survive today.

The Jaguar Throne

This stone throne is one of many jaguar images found at Chichen Itza. The Mayan kings linked themselves with the jaguar, which was the most feared animal in the South American jungle.

The Great Ball Court

Ball courts have been found in several Mayan cities. We do not know the rules of the game but many historians think that players had to pass a rubber ball through stone hoops set high in the wall. Decorations on the court walls suggest the games had some religious meaning and they could have involved human sacrifice.

Hoop

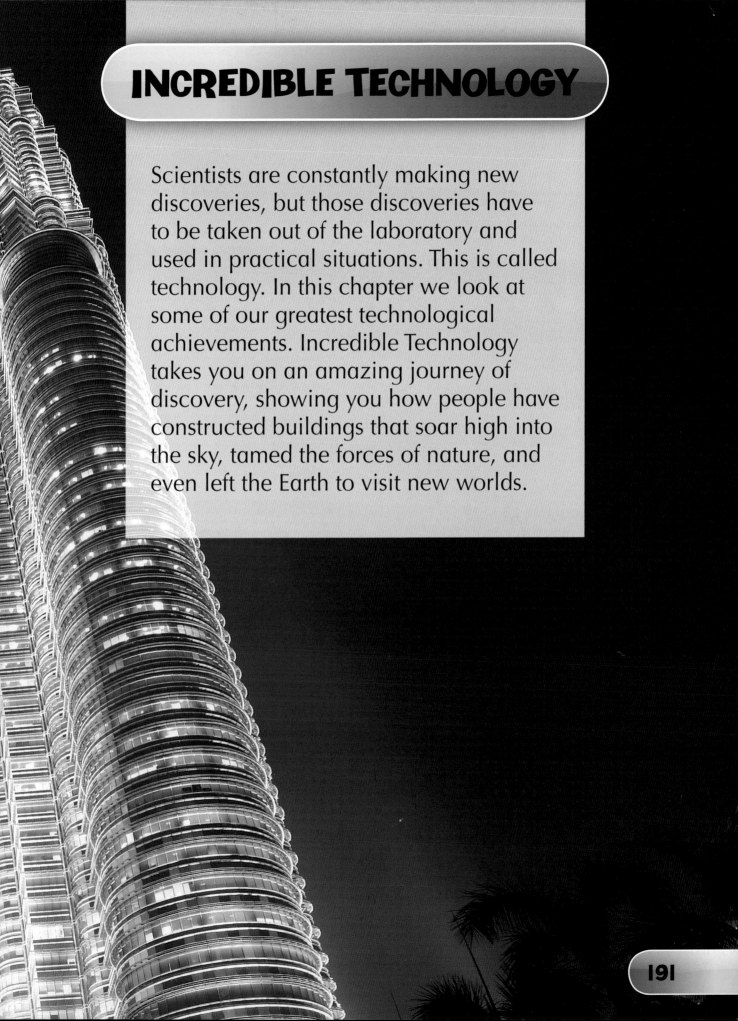

INCREDIBLE TECHNOLOGY

Scientists are constantly making new discoveries, but those discoveries have to be taken out of the laboratory and used in practical situations. This is called technology. In this chapter we look at some of our greatest technological achievements. Incredible Technology takes you on an amazing journey of discovery, showing you how people have constructed buildings that soar high into the sky, tamed the forces of nature, and even left the Earth to visit new worlds.

The London Eye

The London Eye became the world's largest passenger-carrying wheel when it opened in 2000. On a clear day you can see for 25 miles, taking in all the capital's landmarks and the countryside beyond.

The wheel

The London Eye may look like a large bicycle wheel with 80 spokes, but its size presented the designers with problems. A lot of the construction work was done with the wheel lying flat on pontoon bridges in the River Thames. When it was completed, the wheel was lifted upright using cranes.

The Eye has 32 capsules made of curved glass, each of them able to hold up to 25 people. During the ride, passengers can walk around inside the capsule to enjoy the views of London. A round trip is a journey of only around a quarter of a mile, but it lasts 30 minutes. Passengers get on and off while the wheel is moving.

Top Facts

- The London Eye is 443 feet high, almost 130 feet taller than Big Ben, which is nearby.

- The passengers can barely feel the wheel moving. It moves at a speed of one third of a mile per hour.

Atlantic
Ocean

**UNITED
KINGDOM**

London •

Europe

Millennium celebrations

The London Eye was built after its designers won a competition for a structure that would celebrate the millennium. It was only intended to stay in place for five years after it opened on December 31, 1999. However, it soon became Britain's most popular visitor attraction, and its future is now guaranteed for at least another 20 years.

The Eden Project

The Eden Project in Cornwall, UK, has the world's largest greenhouse. Around 100,000 plants from around the world grow in huge plastic domes. There are three areas called biomes, each with a different climate.

Inside the domes

One of the biomes contains plants and trees that live in tropical rain forests (below). The air here is warm and damp. The second biome contains plants that live farther away from the Equator, in places such as the Mediterranean (left). The third biome is an open-air space, which has plants that grow in the UK and countries with similar climates.

Top Facts

- Rainwater is used to water the plants. On average, enough water to fill 20,000 baths is collected every day.
- In 2007 the world's first mechanical theater opened at the Eden Project. Life-size robots act out plays about the environment.

UNITED KINGDOM

Eden Project •

Europe

Did You Know?

The Eden Project's aim is to explain how important it is to take care of the environment. We must look after the world's natural resources so that there is a secure future for all the species that live on the planet.

Covering the domes

The plastic sheets that cover the domes are a hundred times lighter than glass, and they are self-cleaning. On cold days air is pumped between the sheets, which acts like a blanket and keeps the dome warm.

Great bridges

Most modern bridges are elegant suspension bridges. They can span enormous distances and are cheaper to build than other types of bridge. Thick cables are stretched between tall towers made from steel or concrete. Smaller cables attached to these hold up the deck of the bridge.

The Golden Gate Bridge

The Golden Gate Bridge across San Francisco Bay is around 1½ miles long and was the world's largest suspension bridge when it opened in 1937. The steel towers that support the two main cables are over 700 feet high. The cables are nearly 3 feet thick, and contain over 25,000 separate wires.

Did You Know?

Suspension bridges look rigid but they are constantly moving. They are designed to cope with high winds and heavy rain, as well as the weight of the traffic.

The Oresund Bridge

Oresund Bridge links two countries, Sweden and Denmark, carrying trains and vehicles across the Oresund Strait. The railroad track runs underneath a four-lane road. The bridge is linked to a tunnel, which carries traffic from Copenhagen, the capital of Denmark, to the Swedish city of Malmö. Oresund Bridge is nearly 5 miles long.

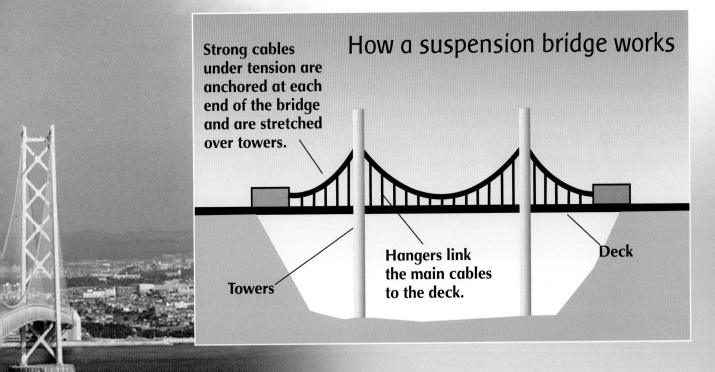

How a suspension bridge works

Strong cables under tension are anchored at each end of the bridge and are stretched over towers.

Hangers link the main cables to the deck.

Towers

Deck

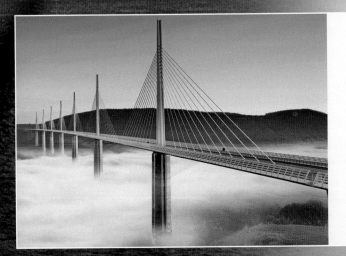

The Millau Bridge

Millau Bridge in France is the world's highest vehicle-carrying bridge. The River Tarn is 886 feet below the deck of the bridge. Seven concrete pylons support the bridge, with 295-foot columns on top of each of them. The tallest column rises 1,125 feet from the floor of the valley, making it higher than the Eiffel Tower.

The Reichstag Dome

Berlin has been the home of Germany's parliament since the divided country was reunified in 1990. To mark this historic event a magnificent new glass dome was added to the 100-year-old Reichstag, or parliament, building. British architect Norman Foster designed the dome, which was completed in 1999.

The Dome

The dome is an amazing steel and glass structure, 130 feet wide and 75 feet tall. The dome plays an important role in the building's heating and ventilation system. Hot air is removed from the top of the dome, but before this happens the energy is extracted.

The central feature of the dome is an amazing structure made up of 360 mirrors, shaped like an upside down cone. During the day, the mirrors reflect light into the chamber below. At night, the mirrors reflect the artificial light inside the chamber to the outside. The dome becomes like a lighthouse, showing the people of Berlin that their parliament is meeting.

Inside the chamber

Germany's parliament is called the Bundestag and has 614 members. Visitors can sit in the gallery above the Bundestag's chamber and listen to the discussions of the parliament.

Did You Know?

A sun shield prevents people from being blinded by the sun's rays coming through the dome. The shield follows the movement of the sun automatically.

A spiraling ramp leads up to a roof terrace.

The Guggenheim Museum, Bilbao

The Guggenheim Museum in Bilbao, Spain, isn't just a building, it's an amazing limestone, glass, and metal sculpture. It is covered with 30,000 sheets of titanium. These look like fish scales, which suits the building's riverside setting. The museum took five years to design and build and was completed in 1997.

Top Facts

• The glass used in the museum walls has a special coating, which lets in light but protects the exhibits from the heat.

• The building covers 58,000 square feet —that's the size of four soccer pitches.

Crazy shapes

The shape of the building is so complicated that architect Frank Gehry's design would have been almost impossible to draw without the help of a computer. Some of the museum's 19 galleries are simple rectangular shapes, while others have no right-angled corners or flat walls.

Atlantic Ocean

Europe

Bilbao

SPAIN

Mediterranean Sea

Inside the museum

The galleries are built around a central space. They are linked by curved walkways and glass lifts. The main gallery, shown here, is 425 feet long and 98 feet wide, the largest in the world.

The Burj Al Arab Hotel

The Burj Al Arab Hotel was designed by Tom Wright to look like an Arab sailing boat called a *dhow*. To achieve that aim the hotel was built on a manmade island 300 yards off the shore of Dubai in the Persian Gulf.

Seven-star hotel

Hotels are usually rated up to a maximum of five stars, though some have given themselves six-star status. Burj Al Arab decided to go one better and call itself the world's only seven-star hotel.

The helicopter pad that projects from the building over 500 feet above the ground became the world's highest tennis court when top stars Roger Federer and André Agassi played a match on it.

Did You Know?

The hotel has a seafood restaurant built around a shark-infested aquarium. You have to take a mock submarine ride to reach the restaurant.

Wonderful interiors

The 590-foot-high entrance lobby is the largest in the world. The hotel has just 202 rooms, far fewer than most big hotels. That's because each suite is huge. The largest is 8,400 square feet, around the size of three tennis courts. It even has its own movie theater. The hotel is decorated with the finest gold leaf, marble, granite, and crystal.

Cooling off

The hotel has luxurious indoor and outdoor swimming pools, and even its own beach.

Three Gorges Dam

Three Gorges Dam is the biggest in the world. It lies across China's longest river, the Yangtze, in the central province of Hubei. The dam was built on a stretch of water where the river passes through a series of steep canyons called Three Gorges.

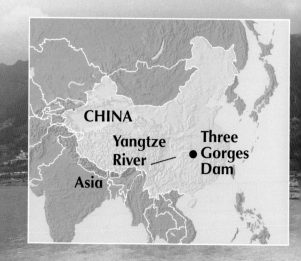

CHINA
Yangtze River — Three Gorges Dam
Asia

Building the dam

The main dam wall is an astounding 7,500 feet long and 590 feet high, and was finished in 2006. The power turbines and lifts are still being installed and the project should be complete in 2009.

The environmental cost

The damming of the river has created a reservoir from flooded land that is over 370 miles long. This farmland was very fertile, and it was also home to some rare animal species such as the Yangtze dolphin and the giant panda. Hundreds of towns and villages have disappeared because of the flooding, and over a million people have had to move to new homes.

Powering China

Three Gorges Dam will be the world's largest hydroelectric power station. Thirty-two generators will supply up to 10 percent of China's electricity needs. This clean, renewable energy source should mean that China won't need to generate so much electricity from coal-burning power stations.

Top Facts

- Water pressure is greater the deeper you go, so dams have to be especially strong at the base. The concrete is 377 feet thick at the base of the dam and only 130 feet thick at the top.

- The three gorges are called Wu, Xiling, and Qutang.

Petronas Towers

Petronas Towers in Kuala Lumpur, Malaysia, are the world's tallest twin towers. The towers are 1,483 feet high to the tip of the spire, and the two-story skybridge that links them at the 42nd floor is the highest of its kind in the world.

Building the towers

Two different companies built the towers and had a race to see who could finish first. It was close until one of the teams found that their tower wasn't quite straight! The tower was only about an inch off vertical, but they lost time putting it right. The 190-foot bridge that links the towers was constructed on the ground and then lifted into position on giant cranes. If there was a fire in one of the towers, people could use the bridge to get out of the building safely.

Inside the towers

At ground level the towers are joined to form a large shopping and entertainment area, built around a central atrium. There is an 880-seat concert hall, an art gallery, and a library. The towers have double-decker elevators. The lower deck takes passengers to the odd-numbered floors, while the upper deck stops at the even-numbered floors above.

Did You Know?

Claiming the title of "world's tallest building" has caused arguments about how a building is measured. The rule is that spires count, because they are part of the design. Masts and flagpoles don't count.

Asia

Kuala Lumpur

Indian Ocean

MALAYSIA

Top Facts

- The towers have 32,000 windows. It takes a team of window cleaners two months to clean them.

- A Frenchman called Alain Robert has tried to climb the outside of Petronas Towers twice. Each time the police have stopped him.

The CN Tower

The CN Tower in Toronto, Canada, is the tallest free-standing structure in the world. It is 1,815 feet from the ground to the top of the antenna. CN stands for Canadian National, the railway company that built the tower.

View from the top

The tower has 1,776 steps, the world's longest staircase. Glass-fronted elevators take visitors up the outside of the building in under a minute. At 1,122 feet there is a deck with a glass floor. Above that there is a revolving restaurant, which takes 72 minutes to rotate. Another lift takes people to the Sky Pod, from where this picture is taken. It is the world's highest observation deck, 1,466 feet above the ground.

Comparing heights

Great Pyramid
Giza, Egypt
452 feet

Eiffel Tower
Paris, France
1,063 feet

Empire State Building
New York, USA
1,453 feet

Petronas Towers
Kuala Lumpur, Malaysia
1,483 feet

CN Tower
Toronto, Canada
1,815 feet

CANADA

Pacific
Ocean

Toronto

North
America

Top Facts

- The tower was built by pouring concrete into a metal container, like a Jell-o mold. When the concrete set, the container was raised and the process was repeated.

- The glass floor on the 1,122-foot deck is 2½ inches thick, and strong enough to take the weight of 14 hippopotamuses.

Did You Know?

Lightning strikes the tower around 50 times a year on average. The building is protected by copper strips, which conduct the lightning safely down the side of the building to the ground.

Cape Canaveral and the Kennedy Space Center

Cape Canaveral is America's main base for launching rockets into space. It is run by NASA, which stands for the National Aeronautics and Space Administration.

Did You Know?
Cape Canaveral's telephone code is 3-2-1 —just like a countdown!

The Kennedy Space Center

In 1961 President John F. Kennedy announced that America intended to put a man on the Moon. A large launch site was needed and NASA decided the best place for it was next to Cape Canaveral. The new site was named the Kennedy Space Center in honor of the president. The Rocket Garden at the Kennedy Space Center (above) is a museum about space exploration. Visitors can see the rockets that blasted the first American astronauts into space, and sit in an *Apollo* capsule to see just how cramped it is.

UNITED STATES OF AMERICA

Atlantic Ocean

State of Florida

Cape Canaveral

Gulf of Mexico

The Space Shuttle

The first Space Shuttle was launched from the Kennedy Space Center in 1981. The Shuttle uses rocket power to travel into space, and lands like a glider when it returns to Earth. The earlier *Apollo* capsules floated down on parachutes and had to be fished out of the Pacific Ocean.

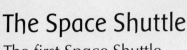

Men on the Moon

The Kennedy Space Center has a place in history because it was from there that the rocket *Apollo 11* was launched. *Apollo 11* was the the first manned rocket to land on the Moon. The astronauts Neil Armstrong (left) and Buzz Aldrin (right) were the first people to walk on the Moon, while Michael Collins (center) stayed on the spacecraft orbiting it.

The Hoover Dam

The Colorado River regularly flooded the southwestern states of America until the Hoover Dam, named after President Herbert Hoover, was built. The dam stands 725 feet high and was the largest ever built when it was completed in 1935.

State of Nevada

Hoover Dam

Pacific Ocean

State of Arizona

UNITED STATES OF AMERICA

Powering the south-west

It took 4,000 men four years to build the Hoover Dam. It was built using concrete blocks that were 5 feet high and up to 59 feet long, locked together like a giant Lego set. Water from the dam produces enough electricity for over a miiiion people.

Top Facts

- The Hoover Dam was the first manmade structure to use more building blocks than the Egyptian pyramids.

- The dam lies on the border between Arizona and Nevada, which is marked by a white line. You can stand with each foot in a different state.

Lake Mead

The dam created one of the world's biggest manmade lakes. Lake Mead is over 62 miles long and provides drinking water for around 25 million people. Every year millions of people use the lake for swimming, boating, diving, and fishing. If the water level in the lake rises, it can't go over the top of the dam because there is an overflow, just like in a bathtub or sink. This has happened once, when Lake Mead flooded in 1983.

Did You Know?

The concrete used to build the dam was poured in stages because it produces heat as it sets. If the concrete had been poured all in one go it would have taken 125 years to set.

The Panama Canal

The Panama Canal connects the Atlantic and Pacific Oceans. Before it was built, ships crossing the globe had to travel round the tip of South America, thousands of miles out of their way.

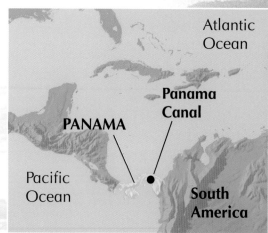

Building the canal

In 1880 a French team started work on the canal in Panama, which was chosen because only a narrow strip of land divides the two oceans. The French gave up after 10 years because of disease and landslides. America took over the project and the canal was completed in 1914.

Locks

The locks on the canal are nearly 1,000 feet long and over 100 feet wide, which is too small for the largest container ships. Larger locks are being constructed. The canal has three sets of locks, which raise ships over 80 feet and lower them back to sea level at the other end.

Using the canal

It takes around nine hours for a ship to pass through the 50-mile-long canal. Around 40 vessels a day make that journey. Vessels have to pay a toll to pass through the canal and the amount depends on their size. The record amount is $250,000, while Richard Halliburton paid just 36 cents in 1928. He swam through!

Did You Know?

Over 25,000 people lost their lives during the canal's construction. Many of them died from malaria, a disease carried by mosquitoes.

GLOSSARY

Amphibian
Animal able to live on land and in water, for example a frog.

Amphitheater
An oval-shaped building in a Roman city, open to the sky, with seats in rows, one above another, around an open space at ground level. Used for staging gladiator fights.

Antarctic
The area around the South Pole.

Archaeologist
A person who studies the remains of past civilizations.

Architect
A person who designs buildings.

Arctic
The region that surrounds the North Pole.

Arctic Circle
An imaginary line around the North Pole which marks the area that experiences 24-hour darkness in midwinter.

Asthma
A disease of the lungs that is often caused by allergies and leads to coughing and difficulties in breathing.

Astronaut
A person who travels in space.

Atrium
A large open space within a modern building, usually more than one story high with large windows or a glass roof. In a Roman house the atrium is a central courtyard and has no roof.

Aurora
Colorful display of lights high in Earth's atmosphere. They are caused by charged particles from the Sun reacting with gases in the atmosphere.

Bazaar
A market place in a middle eastern country.

Biome
A large community of plants and animals such as a forest, grassland, or desert.

Camouflage
A disguise used by some animals to blend in with their surroundings. Some animals are the same color as the plants or rocks in their habitat and some can change their color when they are in danger.

Canal
A long, narrow manmade strech of water, often used to transport heavy materials, such as coal, by boat.

Canyon
A deep river valley with steep sides.

Cathedral
The main Christian church in an area.

Chamber
A large room used for meetings, often where a parliament meets.

Circumference
The outer line of a circle or the length of that line.

Civilization
An advanced society that has towns, art, religion, writing, and money.

Climate
The pattern of weather in an area.

Continent
One of Earth's seven large land areas, which are Africa, Asia, Australasia, Europe, North America, South America, and Antarctica.

Convict Ship
A ship which transported people found guilty of crimes. Many criminals were transported from England to Australia in the 1800s.

Crater
The mouth of a volcano from which the lava surfaces. Also a wide hollow in the ground caused by an explosion or something heavy hitting the ground.

Desert
An area of land that receives little or no rain during the year.

Delta
Where a river meets the sea. The river drops stones and mud to create a triangular system of small river chanels that make up the delta.

Embassy
The building in which an ambassador, the representative of a foreign government, and his or her staff work.

Empire
Many different lands or counties ruled over by one leader.

Engineer
A person trained to design and build machinery or roads and bridges.

Equator
The imaginary line that runs around Earth halfway between the two poles.

Evaporate
To change from a liquid into a gas, for instance when liquid water turns into the gas water vapor.

Evolve
To undergo changes from one generation to the next, a process that very gradually improves a species.

Fossil
Evidence of a dead animal or plant, which has been preserved in rock or another substance, such as amber. Fossils are usually millions of years old.

Glider
An aircraft without an engine which flies by floating on warm air currents.

Gravity
The force that pulls everything on Earth toward its center.

Habitat
The type of place where an animal or plant lives.

Hemisphere
One half of Earth. The Northern Hemisphere lies north of the Equator and the Southern Hemisphere lies south of it.

Hibernation
A deep sleep that some animals go into to survive the winter. Their heart rate slows down and the animals appear to be dead.

Hydroelectric power
Electricity created by the movement of water. Water flows over a turbine causing it to spin. The turbine is connected to a generator and the spinning motion creates electricity.

Immigrant
A person who comes into a foreign country to live there permanently.

Junk
Chinese boat with a flat bottom and square sails.

Legend
A story that has been told for many, many years, passed down through generations of people. A legend may be true or untrue.

Lent
The 40-day period leading up to Easter Day. Christians traditionally fast (eat very little) during Lent.

Lock
In a canal, an area where the water level can be raised or lowered by opening gates to allow a boat to travel up or down a hill.

Magma
The molten (liquid) rock under the surface of Earth that rises up through volcanoes.

Medieval
Belong to or to do with the Middle Ages, the period between about A.D. 1100 and 1500.

Migration
The movement of animals or people from one region to another.

Minaret
A tall slender tower on or beside a mosque.

Minerals
Substances that are found naturally in rocks or in earth, such as metals, coal, and salt. Some lakes and the Dead Sea have a high mineral content, which makes it difficult for animals and plants to live in the water.

Monsoon
A seasonal wind that blows in one direction for six months and then reverses its direction for the other six months. The Indian monsoon blows from land to the sea during the winter months. In summer, it blows in the opposite direction, bringing heavy, cooling rains off the Indian Ocean.

Monument
A statue or building built to celebrate or remind people of an important person or event.

Mosaic
A design, often found on Roman floors, made from small pieces of stone or tile.

Mosque
A Muslim place of worship.

Mythology
Traditional stories that have been made up to explain natural events, such as the movements of the Sun and Moon in the sky, or to give reasons for religious beliefs.

Nirvana
The state of perfect happiness in the Buddhist religion.

North Pole
The northernmost point on the Earth's surface.

Oasis
A small area in a desert where water is found and plants can easily grow.

Observatory
A building or a room containing a telescope which is used to view the stars and planets.

Orbit
The path of one body in space around another, for example a spacecraft can orbit the Moon or the Moon can orbit the Earth.

Parliament
The group of elected representatives who meet to make the laws for a country.

Philosopher
Someone who studies questions of existence, knowledge, and behavior.

Pontoon bridge
A row of flat-bottomed boats or floating objects used to make a temporary bridge.

Pylon
A strong towerlike structure used as a support. Pylons are often made of metal and used to support power lines. Also a gateway to an Ancient Egyptian temple.

Rainforest
A dense kind of forest found in areas with high rainfall. Rainforests are usually found near to the Equator.

Reservoir
A manmade lake that is built to store water. This water can either be used for drinking or it can be chaneled through turbines that are connected to a generator to produce electricity.

Sacrifice
An offering to please a god, usually food or an animal. In some ancient cultures a person was killed as a sacrifice.

Sandstone
A rock formed from sand.

Scroll
A roll of paper or parchment usually with writing or pictures on it.

Shrine
A place of worship linked with a sacred person.

Skyline
The outline of buildings or land seen against the sky.

South Pole
The southernmost point on the Earth's surface.

Species
A group of animals or plants that are very similar, such as humans, dogs, or grasses.

Sphinx
An Ancient Egyptian statue with the body of a lion and the head of a human, often a king.

Stalactite
A hardened, icicle shaped lump formed from calcium and other minerals which grows down from the roof of a cave.

Strait
A narrow channel of water between two seas or oceans.

Suburb
A district on the outskirts of a city where many people live.

Terracotta
A mixture of clay and sand used to make statues or pottery.

Titanium
A silver or gray colored light-weight metal which does not rust.

Tornado
A narrow column of violently spinning air. The powerful winds in a tornado blow at speeds of around 300 miles per hour.

Turbine
A set of angled blades that spins when water or air flows over it. Turbines are often attached to generators, which turn the spinning motion of the blades into electricity.

INDEX

ACKNOWLEDGEMENTS

Photo credits:

b = bottom, t = top, r = right, l = left, c = center

Cover images:

Front: tl Brian A. Vikander/CORBIS, tc Will & Deni McIntyre/GettyImages,
tr Carson Ganci/Design Pics/CORBIS, c Theo Allofs/zefa/CORBIS,
bl Martin Harvey/CORBIS, br Image Plan/CORBIS.
Back: tl Larry Lee Photography/CORBIS, tr Joseph Sohm/Visions of America/CORBIS,
bc Free Agents Limited/CORBIS.
Spine: Brian A. Vikander/CORBIS.

Internal images:

CORBIS
2-3, 4-5, 6-7, 10-11, 12-13, 12, 13, 14-15, 15t, 16-17, 16, 17b, 19t, 20, 20, 21, 22-23, 22, 23t,
23b, 24-25, 25t, 25b, 26-27, 27t, 27b, 28-29, 28, 30-31, 30t, 30b, 31, 33t, 34-35, 36-37, 37b,
38-39, 38, 39, 40-41, 40, 41, 42-43, 43t, 43b, 45t, 45bl, 48-49, 48, 49, 50, 54-55, 55t, 55b, 56-57,
57t, 57b, 59t, 62-63, 64-65, 66-67, 67t, 67b, 71t, 71b,72-73, 73t, 73b, 74-75, 74, 75t, 78-89, 79t,
80-81, 81t, 82-83, 82, 83t, 83b, 84-85, 84, 85t, 85b, 88-89, 88t, 89t, 89b, 91t, 92-93, 93t, 94-95,
95t, 95b, 96-97, 97t, 97b, 98-99, 98, 99t, 99b, 102, 103l, 104-105, 104, 105r, 105l, 106-107,
106l, 106r, 107, 108-109, 108, 109, 100, 110-111, 110, 111, 114-115, 114, 115r, 116-117, 116t,
116b, 117, 118-119, 118, 119t, 119b, 120-121, 120, 121t, 121b, 122-123, 122, 123t, 123b,
124-125, 124, 125t, 126, 126-127, 126, 127t, 127b, 128-129, 128, 130-131, 130t, 131, 132-
133,133t, 133b, 134-135, 134, 135t, 135b, 136, 137 (background), 137t, 137b, 138-139, 140,
141t, 143(background), 144-145, 144, 145t, 145b,146-147, 147, 148 (background), 148l,
150-151, 150, 151t, 152-153, 153b, 154-155, 154, 155t, 156-157, 157b,158, 159t, 159b, 159
(background), 160-161, 161, 162-163, 163t, 163b, 164-165, 166-167, 168, 168-169, 168, 169t,
169b, 170-171, 171l, 172-173, 172l, 172r, 173, 174-175, 174, 176 (background), 177
(background),177t, 177r, 178-179, 178t, 178b, 180-181, 180, 181t, 181b, 182-183, 182b,182t,
183, 184-185, 184, 185t, 185b, 186-187, 187tr, 187b, 188-189, 189br, 190-191, 192, 192-193,
194t, 194b, 196-197, 196, 197t, 197b, 198-199, 198, 199, 200, 201, 202-203, 203t, 203b,
204-205, 204l, 205, 206-207, 206, 207, 208-209, 208, 210-211, 211t, 211b, 212-213, 212, 213,
214, 215, 216-217

GETTY IMAGES
1, 8-9, 10, 11t, 15b, 17t, 18-19, 19b, 29b, 32-33, 32, 33b, 34-35, 37t, 46-47, 47t, 47b, 58-59, 58,
59b, 65b, 62, 63t, 63b, 66, 68-69, 68t, 68b, 69, 70-71, 70, 75b, 78, 80, 86-87, 90-91, 91b,
100-101, 101, 102-103, 103r, 112-113, 115l, 129, 125b, 143t, 143b, 146, 149 (background) 149,
151b, 153t, 157t, 160, 166, 167, 171r, 175, 179, 187tl, 193, 195, 200-201, 202, 204r, 210

ISTOCKPHOTO
11b

DIGITAL VISION
29, 45br, 51, 52-53, 53t, 53b, 60-61, 76-77, 76, 77tr, 77tl, 81

GNP
93b, 94, 141(background), 141b, 142, 154b